AIKIDO
Tradition and New Tomiki
Free Fighting Method

By Nobuyoshi Higashi

Disclaimer

Although both Unique Publications and the author(s) of this martial arts book have taken great care to ensure the authenticity of the information and techniques contained herein, we are not responsible, in whole or in part, for any injury which may occur to the reader or readers by reading and/or following the instructions in this publication. We also do not guarantee that the techniques and illustrations described in this book will be safe and effective in a self-defense or training situation. It is understood that there exist a potential for injury when using or demonstrating the techniques herein described. It is essential that before following any of the activities, physical or otherwise, herein described, the reader or readers first should consult his or her physician for advice on whether practicing or using the techniques described in this publication could cause injury, physical or otherwise. Since the physical activities described herein could be too sophisticated in nature for the reader or readers, it is essential a physician be consulted. Also, federal, state or local laws may prohibit the use or possession of weapons described herein. A thorough examination must be made of the federal, state and local laws before the reader or readers attempts to use these weapons in a self-defense situation or otherwise. Neither Unique Publications nor the author(s) of this martial arts book guarantees the legality or the appropriateness of the techniques or weapons herein contained.

ISBN: 0-86568-144-9

 **UNIQUE PUBLICATIONS**
4201 Vanowen Place
Burbank, CA 91505

Contents

AIKIDO
Tradition and New Tomiki Free Fighting Method

BY NOBUYOSHI HIGASHI, B.A, M.A. President, Kokushi Budo Institute of New York, Inc. Assistant Professor, State University of New York at Stony Brook. 6th Degree (aikido, and karate), 7th Degree (judo), and 8th Degree Black Belt (jujitsu). The Author of School Judo, Kokushi-ryu Jujitsu, Basic Judo, and Karate-do. President, the United States Tomiki Aikido Association.

Kokushi Budo Institute of New York, Inc.

Preface

I met Professor Kenji Tomiki in 1960. I held a 4th degree black belt in judo and was preparing for the Judo Championship. Professor Magokichi Ueno, who was the head judo coach, introduced Professor Kenji Tomiki to us. He told us the "Professor Tomiki is going to teach everyone aikido after the judo practice." We didn't like the idea, because we practiced judo for over two hours, after which everybody was always tired. But we learned aikido. I was impressed by his great instruction and the effectiveness of his joint techniques. He told us, "I have been studying judo since I was 10 years old and aikido for over 30 years so that my research has focused on the relationship between judo and aikido. I always think with a judo mind to evaluate the aikido techniques. Judo players should learn aikido, because the principle of Tomiki aikido is based on Judo."

I received my second impression of Professor Tomiki at the meeting of the philosophy division of All Japan Physical Education Association in 1961. At that time, he was the leader of this association, and I was a new member of the philosophy division. At the meeting, Professor Tomiki explained the philosophy behind aikido especially the role of body movement, such as using minimum power to get maximum results. He demonstrated Ushiro-ryote-mochi (rear both hands grasp). We were impressed by his application of off-balance techniques without using strength. After this meeting, I read Professor Tomiki's articles and books and decided to study aikido seriously.

Many years later, on a very hot day in August of 1979. My wife and I met Professor Tomiki at the aikido dojo of the Kokushikan University. We studied with him all morning and late into the afternoon without a break for lunch. There were no open windows, and I believe that the temperature was close to 100 degrees; but he never stopped teaching aikido. I was worried about his health because he was almost 80 years old. Finally I asked that we please rest for a moment. Tomiki responded saying, "You have only one day to practice aikido because you have to go back to New York. On the other hand, I want to teach you as many techniques as I can so that you can teach Tomiki Aikido in the United States." So we sat down, and he started to teach us the philosophy of aikido. Then we discussed the future development of aikido throughout the world. After the practice, Professor Tomiki asked about aikido in the United States. I explained that there are only a few schools practicing aikido there, but I introduced aikido as a physical education course at State University of New York at Stony Brook.

He was very happy to hear that. Then he said that as long as a person practices Tomiki Aikido, he will be happy. I respected and admired Professor Tomiki very much, and I hoped that I would teach like him when I reach his age. Professor Tomiki was a very busy man, but whenever I was in Tokyo, he always took time to teach me aikido.

When we were about to leave Tokyo, I spoke to my teacher saying, "See you in a few years. Please take care of your health, and good luck." He said that people need a new aikido and told me to teach and develop Tomiki Aikido in the Unites States. We left Tokyo the next day. Four months later, Professor Tomiki died. I thought then that perhaps Professor Tomiki wanted to teach us so much because he foresaw the end of his life. With his death we lost a great man. Nevertheless, his philosophy and aikido have continued to develop. And now we are going to continue to advance Tomiki Aikido as long as we live.

I wish to thank the following advanced black belt students for assistance in helping me to finish this book: Instructor Satomi Higashi, demonstration partner Mr. Wesley E. Freeburg, Ms. Tomomi Seki Freeburg, Photographer Ms. Robin M. Rosenthal, and the students who contributed to this book in so many ways.

I. What is Aikido?

Aikido is an art directed toward the coordination of your body rhythm and movements with those of your opponent, and it develops an efficient use of mind and body.   It involves the physical skills of power, speed, coordination, and movement perception.

Technically, you attack your opponent's physiologically weak structural points, such as the vital spots and joints of the human body, as well as the dynamic weak points, such as the opponent's balance (i.e., when the opponent's balance is in flux.) For example, if your opponent is bigger than you and pushes against your chest, you will naturally lose your balance and fall down. But if, when the same opponent pushes you, your feet and body move backward faster than you are pushed, your opponent will lose balance in direct relation to the exertion of his/her own strength, and may even fall down. If at this time you apply the techniques of Aikido, you need only the minimum of effort to achieve maximum results. Another example: When your opponent strikes at your face with his/her fist, you can avoid this blow by turning your body to either the left or the right so that the opponent will miss you, leaving his/her arm extended (a position I call "dead of power"). At this time, it is easy to grasp the opponent and apply one of the techniques of the art. To take the advantage successfully, you must know your opponent's speed, attacking pattern, and direction of movement.

Generally, the practice of Aikido presupposes non-resistance theory, non-violence, and non-aggression; it is an art that cultivates spirit and beauty.

By practicing methods of both attack and defense, you train to control your opponent without harm. You learn to move harmoniously, responding to the opponent's power and movements, in order to achieve maximum efficiency. You learn to use your opponent's strength for your own advantage. Developing self-confidence and self-discipline , you become strong in both mind and body.

The practice of Aikido is more than a physical activity or sport. A look at the meaning of the word "Aikido" shows that. Aikido is, in fact, a philosophy of life.

"Ai" is harmony, togetherness, blending, and love, including harmony between persons, with nature, and world harmony. The realization of ai means that you love other people and do not turn against them. It means that you follow the laws of nature and live at one with all things.

"Ki" represents two kinds of power. I would describe ki as both the power of the human being and the power inherent in nature. The human ki is the source of human power; and it develops together with the mind and body. For example, when you are afraid of your opponent, your power moves away from your internal body and is lost to you; but if you develop fearlessness or courage, ki will build in your entire body. The feeling of ki transforms human power, so you should develop this positive, strong feeling. You should feel that the body is full of a power (ki) that comes from your center of gravity (just below the navel), travels through your fingertips, and extends in the direction of your body movement. Below are several examples of ki development and training.

If your opponent pushes against your chest, you should project your ki to his/her rear, and then your opponent cannot push you back easily because of the opposition provided by your own creative power (ki). Suppose you are not feeling well. If you believe in and develop the feeling of ki, you can overcome illness and eventually get better.

The other ki refers to the power of nature. This concept represents the forces of nature that we cannot control - the sun shining, water running downhill, the force of gravity causing things to fall, etc. We must live in harmony with these forces and follow in the path of nature.

"Do" is the way of life of a human being. Following this path you will never give way to temptation or difficulties, you will strive continuously to attain your object and to win your way to higher forms of happiness, love, and success.

Always live in the midst of human power and the power of nature. Aikido provides the way to blend nature and human power. It is the way of happiness, peace, and love.

II. History of Aikido

Aikido was established by Professor Morihei Ueshiba (1883-1969). He studied older styles of Jujitsu and other martial arts, especially Daito-ryu Aiki Jujitsu, which specializes in th application of joint techniques. He developed a new philosophy and the techniques that later comprised Aikido. In 1931, the Kobukan school was founded. A new Aikikai (Aiki Association) was established in 1948. Since then, Aikido has spread throughout the world.

TOMIKI AIKIDO

Professor Kenji Tomiki was born in Akita prefecture in 1900. He began to learn judo at the age of 10, and continued to practice the art for the rest of his life. Upon completing his elementary and secondary school studies, he received the two highest awards for both academic excellence and achievement in physical education. In 1923, Tomiki matriculated in the Economic Department of the Waseda University from which he graduated in 1927. During his college years, the young Kenji Tomiki met Dr. Jigoro Kano (the founder of judo) and received personal instruction from him. Professor Tomiki's form of aikido was, thus, influenced by Dr. Kano's philosophy and education as well as master Ueshiba's mastery and knowledge of aikido.

About this time, Professor Tomiki held a 5th degree black belt and was known to be one of the greatest judo players. He began to study aikido with master Morihei Ueshiba in 1926. Professor Tomiki was deeply impressed by the beautiful and skillful techniques of Ueshiba's aikido. Therefore, he learned as much as he could from him. In 1927, Master Morihei Ueshiba opened an aikido club in what had formerly been the billiard room of Prince Shimazu's mansion. Professor Tomiki was the manager (kanji) and assistant of his organization during the time he studied aikido with Master Ueshiba.

Tomiki represented the Miyagi prefecture in the Special Judo Competition (Tenran Budo Taikai), which determined the judo championship for all Japan. During the competition, he broke his rib and was unable to participate in the finals. After that, he retired from judo competition.

In 1931, he took a job as a junior high school teacher in the Akita prefecture. In 1936, when the Daidogakuen School was opened in Manchuria (China), he took a teaching position there. In 1938, the Manchurian National Kenkoku University was established, and Professor Tomiki was invited to teach the martial arts (aikido and judo) there.

Ueshiba's training of aikido emphasized form practice. For example, whenever the student strikes or grasps you, you must apply the appropriate technique. Professor Tomiki earned the 8th degree black belt and was, therefore, the first person to receive the highest degree from Master Ueshiba. After he received the highest degree, he did research and studied by himself and gradually came to believe that aikido needs a free practice like judo free practice in order to develop more effective techniques. During this Manchurian period, while studying and teaching aikido, he conceived the idea of the present 17 techniques of kihon-no-kata.

At the time, when Japan lost World War II, Professor Tomiki was a professor at Kenkoku University in China. Therefore, he was taken to Siberia as a prisoner of the Soviet Army. He remained in a detention camp for about 3 years, after which he was able to return to Japan in 1948. He joined the Kodokan Judo Institute as an instructor and as a leader of the judo organization. In the same year, he became instructor in the physical education department of Waseda University. Between 1950 and 1979, he was a member of the Board of the All Japan Judo Association. In 1951, he became a head coach of judo at Waseda University during that time, he taught aikido to the judo students there. He separated the aikido club from the judo club, founding Waseda Aikido Club in 1958. At this time, aikido was first recognized by Waseda University as a part of its physical education program.

At that time, atemi-waza and kansetsu-waza (except for elbow joint techniques) were not included in judo practice, because they were too dangerous for the students. They are, however, very effective and skillful techniques. Professor Tomiki believed that if the rules and methods of the practice were changed, it would prove a good sport and suitable for physical education programs.

He, therefore, researched and studied many techniques and established aiki-randoriho (aiki free practice) around 1959-1960. This he discussed in his article "Waseda hoshiki niyoru aikido no taikeiteki renshuho, Atemi-waza to Kansetsu-waza (Waseda method of aikido practice, the art of attacking the body and the art of joint taking)," published in 1960.

The method of aikido shiai (competition) has been fought without the use of weapons since 1960. For example, you and your opponent face each other in the fighting stance, arms distance apart. Each attacks freely, and whoever manages to throw his partner or take the joint, gets the point. Whoever has the most points after a determined time will be the winner.

In 1966, a new method of aikido shiai was introduced, involving bare hand defense against knife techniques. For example, your opponent holds a knife in his right hand and thrusts it at your chest. If his knife touches you, he gets a point. If you can avoid being touched by his knife and successfully apply the techniques for a predetermined time, you get a point. Next, you hold the knife and attack him. The one who receives the most points in both attacking and defending will be the winner.

Around 1976, the rules for aikido shiai were changed. Points are only awarded to the defender. For example, you must defend yourself from his knife by throwing him or taking a joint, etc.

On February 1, 1989, the rules reverted to the 1966 version, with some modifications.

Presently, the Tomiki Aikido Championships are held annually in Japan. The First International Tomiki Aikido Championship and Festival was held at Nara, Japan on June 18, 1989.

In 1976, the United States Tomiki Aikido Association was established by Nobuyoshi Higashi in New York City.

Professor Tomiki passed away in 1979, but Tomiki aikido continues to develop throughout the world.

III. The Values of Aikido

Through the practice of Aikido, you develop physical fitness, flexibility, strength, and muscular endurance, increase the capacity of the cardiovascular respiratory system, acquire skills for self-defense, add to your safety education, and increase your self-confidence, capacity for leadership, politeness, and intelligence. You develop coordination of mind, spirit, and body, and learn how to relax from the pressures and the tensions of daily living. Eventually fit, and are able to make a contribution of value to the world.

IV. Basic Knowledge

A. The Bow (rei)

The bow is an expression of sincerity, courtesy, and respect for the opponent in practice or daily life. Whenever you enter or leave the exercise hall, you must bow. Bow to each other before and after the practice of Aikido, or whenever you meet other people, parents, instructors, or friends.

There are two forms of bowing: the standing bow and the kneeling bow.

THE STANDING BOW (tachi-rei)

Stand naturally with your heels together. Bend your upper body slowly to about a 45 degree angle. Move your hands from your side to a point above your knees. Hold this position for a few seconds. Always keep your eyes forward and focused on the mat at a point 12 feet in

front of you. Then raise your upper body and move your
hands back to their original position.

THE KNEELING BOW (za-rei)

Your insteps are on the mat with your right big toe over your left big toe. Your hips are placed directly on your heels with your back straight and your hands on your upper legs. Bend your upper body until it is about 5 inches above the mat. Your hands should move from your thighs to the mat directly in front of your knees, about the distance of a fist in front of them. Hold this posture for a few seconds, and then raise your body to the original position.

B. Breakfall (ukemi)

It is necessary to learn the proper form of breakfall so that you fall safely without shock or injury when thrown by your opponent or when you fall down by yourself. There are four basic kinds of breakfall: 1. Falling backward, 2. Falling sideways, 3. Falling forward, and 4. Forward roll.

1. Falling backward
(ushiro-no-ukemi)

<u>LYING POSITION</u>

Lie down on your back, head up, hands raised about 45 degrees above your body. Next, hit the mat hard with both arms (using the entire arm, palms down) at an angle of about 40 degrees away from your body.

STANDING POSITION

Assume a natural stance, raise your arms (palms down) to shoulder height in front of you. Next, bend your knees until your hips are close to your heels. Fall backward. Before your back touches the mat, hit the mat with both your arms (palms down) at about a 40 degree angle. When your back touches the mat, both legs should be extended and raised upward.

2. Falling sideways
   (yoko-no-ukemi)

LYING POSITION

Lying down on your left side, head up. Your legs should be open about a shoulder width apart, knee slightly bent, your left arm on the mat (palm down) about 40 degrees away from your body. Place your right arm above your body. Next, raise your legs and turn your body to the right. At the same time, hit the mat with your right arm (using both the arm and the palm) about 40 degrees away from your body, and drop your legs. Do not cross your legs.

Repeat on the opposite side.

STANDING POSITION

Assume a natural stance. Raise your right arm straight ahead to shoulder height. Next, move your right foot from your right side to your left side (at this time, your right foot passes just in front of your left foot). Bend your left knee until your hip is close to your left heel. Fall down on your right side, and hit the mat with your right arm about 40 degrees away from your body.

Repeat on the opposite side.

3. Falling forward
(mae-ukemi)

<u>KNEELING POSITION</u>

The knees and balls of your feet should be in contact with the mat, and your upper body should be upright and straight. From this position, fall forward. When you reach the mat, hit the mat in front of your face with your hands (palms down) and forearms. At this time, your fingertips should be pointed slightly inward, and your elbows bent outward slightly. Do not touch your stomach to the mat.

STANDING POSITION

Assume a natural stance. Fall forward, following the same method used in the kneeling position. Do not touch the front of your body to the mat. Only the hands, forearms, and, initially, the balls of the feet should make contact.

4. Forward roll (zenpo-kaiten-ukemi)

SQUATTING POSITION

Begin with natural stance; next, take one step forward with your right foot. Assume a squatting position. Place your left hand on the mat in front of your left foot in line with the toes of your right foot. Put your right hand on the mat between your left hand and your right foot with the fingers pointing inward. Turn your head to the left, and roll forward. At the start of the roll, the outer surface of the right arm should be in contact with the mat, followed by your right shoulder, back, left hip, left leg, and right foot. At the completion of the roll, hit the mat with your left arm and hand (palm down). In the final position, your legs should be extended with knees slightly bent. Do not cross your legs.

Repeat on the opposite side.

STANDING POSITION

Stand in the natural stance with your right foot forward. Bend your upper body forward. Next, follow the same instructions as for the squatting position.

Repeat on the opposite side.

C. The distance (maai)

You should always be able to picture in your mind the best way to attack or defend yourself. And the distance between you and your opponent is an important factor in this. The proper distance will enable you to attack easily, while preventing your opponent from doing so. The proper distance, which provides this opportunity, is achieved by facing each other and stretching your right (or left) hands forward so that you almost touch each other's finger tips. When you take one step forward with your right (or left) foot, you can readily apply the techniques on your opponent. This is the best distance for you. Control your position visavis your opponent by keeping the correct distance between you.

When your opponent attacks you, his/her stances are usually the right foot or the left foot forward stance. At this time, your defending stance will also be the right foot or the left foot forward stance. When the distance between you and your opponent is determined, the stances must be coordinated. Those stances are classified as either aigamae or gyakugamae.

Aigamae (regular stance)

Aigamae (regular stance) has two variations:

1. Your opponent is in the right foot forward stance, and you are in the right foot forward stance.

2. Your opponent is in the left foot forward stance, and you are in the left foot forward stance.

Gyakugamae (reverse stance)

Gyakugamae (reverse stance) has two variations:

1. Your opponent is in the right foot forward stance, and you are in the left foot forward stance.

2. Your opponent is in the left foot forward stance, and you are in the right foot forward stance.

D. Eye contact (metsuke)

View your opponent calmly so that you can see him/her from head to foot. Do not stare at your opponent. If you stare at one area only, you may not see another part of the opponent's body and thus enable your opponent to attack you more easily. For example, if you stare at your opponent's right hand, you may not see your opponent's left hand or foot enabling him/her to attack you with that hand or foot.

E. The knife-hand (shuto)

In Aikido, the knife-hand (shuto) extends from the forearm to the base of the fingers. The shuto is used to block an opponent's punch and to apply the defensive counter-techniques, or it is used to attack your opponent.

There are three basic knife-hand positions: 1. Chudan (middle), 2. Jodan (upper), and 3. Gedan (lower).

1. Chudan (middle)

Stretch your right (or left) arm and keep it slightly bent. Place the knife-hand in front at neck level.

2. Jodan (upper)

Jodan is achieved by the same method as the chudan (middle) except that the knife-hand is placed in front of your head.

3. Gedan (lower)

Gedan also resembles the chudan, except that the knife-hand is placed in front of your lower abdomen.

F. The stances (kamae)

The stances prepare you for attack or defense. An opponent can attack you from many different directions; so in each case you have to be physically and mentally prepared to assume the appropriate stance.

There are three basic stances: 1. Mu-gamae (natural stance), 2. Migi-gamae (right stance), and 3. Hidari-gamae (left stance).

1. Mu-gamae (natural stance)

Your feet are about a shoulder width apart. Stand naturally and keep your center of gravity below the navel.

Keep your body weight 50% on each leg. Your eyes should look forward.

2. Migi-gamae (right stance)

You are in the right foot forward stance. You stand naturally and keep your center of gravity below the navel. Keep your body weight 50% on each leg. Your eyes should look forward.

3. Hidari-gamae (left stance)

You are in the left foot forward stance. You stand naturally and keep your center of gravity below the navel. Keep your body weight 50% on each leg. Your eyes should look forward.

G. Foot movement (unsoku)

Your feet must move close to the ground, with toes touching first when they reach the ground. The most important part of the foot movement is to keep your center of gravity and your foot and body movements coordinated harmoniously.

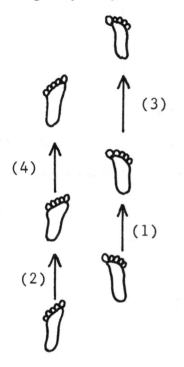

Tsugi-ashi (following feet)

For right tsugi-ashi, advance your right foot forward, and then bring your left foot forward. Your left foot, however, must never pass beyond your right foot. Maintain the right natural stance.

Left tsugi-ashi applies the same principle with the left foot leading and the right foot following.

Ayumi-ashi (ordinary walking feet)

Ayumi-ashi (ordinary walking feet).

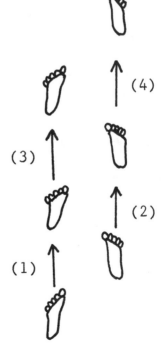

Foot movements include many patterns: front and back; sideways; front sideways and back sideways. The following diagrams illustrate these patterns.

Front and back

1. Move your left foot first.

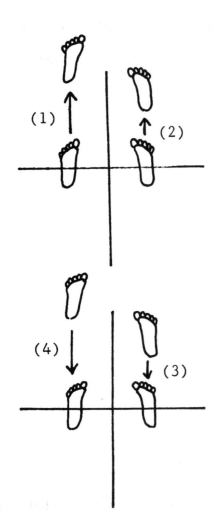

(1)   Advance your left foot then right foot with tsugi-ashi,

(2)   Withdraw your right foot then left foot with tsugi-ashi,

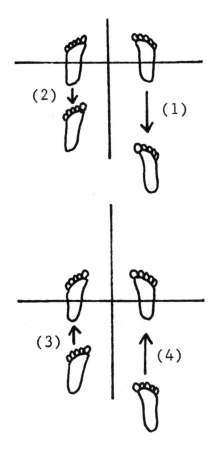

(3)   Withdraw your right foot then left foot with tsugi-ashi,

(4)   Advance your left foot then right foot with tsugi-ashi (beginning position).

2. Move your right foot first.

   Repeat steps 1-4 on the opposite side.

Sideways

1. Move your left foot first.

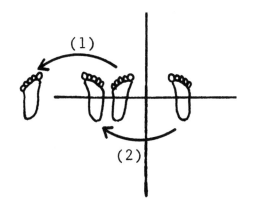

(1)   Move your left foot then right foot to the left,

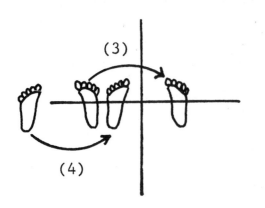

(2)   Move your right foot then left foot to the right,

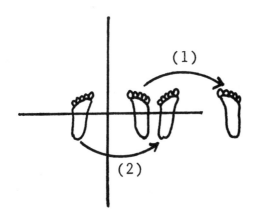

(3)   Move your right foot then left foot to the right,

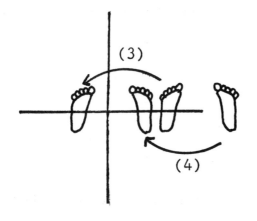

(4)   Move your left foot then right foot to the left (beginning position).

2. Move your right foot first.

     Repeat steps 1-4 on the opposite side.

Front sideways and back sideways

   1. Move your left foot first.

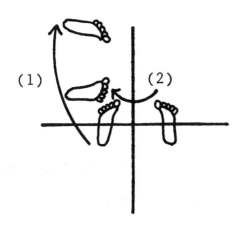

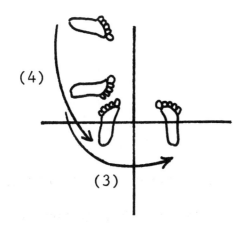

(1)   Advance your left foot then right foot diagonally to the left; simultaneously, turn your body 90 degrees clockwise,

(2)   Advance your right foot then left foot diagonally to the right; at the same time, turn your body 90 degrees counterclockwise (face front),

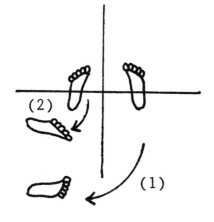

(3)   Withdraw your right foot then left foot diagonally to the left; Simultaneously, turn your body 90 degrees clockwise,

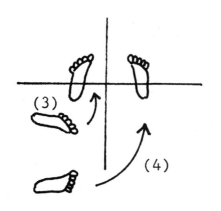

(4)   Advance your left foot then right foot diagonally to the left; at the same time, turn your body 90 degrees counterclockwise (face front).

2. Move your right foot first.

    Repeat steps 1-4 on the opposite side.

H. Off-balance techniques (kuzushi)

Off-balance techniques disturb an opponent's posture by means of pulling or pushing motion. For example, if your opponent pushes against you, you may pull him/her so that he/she loses balance. In other words, you pull or push in the same direction as that of the opponent's force. Pulling and pushing movements are based in body and foot movements so that you attack with the minimum effort required to break the opponent's balance.

There are two ways to disturb your opponent's balance: 1. You force your opponent off-balance by pushing without actually grasping him/her. 2. You force your opponent off-balance by pushing or pulling after grasping him/her.

1. **You force your opponent off-balance by pushing without actually grasping him/her.**

These consist of four ways to upset your opponent's balance: a) Aigamae-koho-kuzushi (regular stance, rear off-balance technique), b) Aigamae-zenpo-kuzushi (regular stance, front off-balance technique), c) Gyakugamae-koho-kuzushi (reverse stance, rear off-balance technique), and d) Gyakugamae-zenpo-kuzushi (reverse stance, front off-balance technique).

a) Aigamae-koho-kuzushi (regular stance, rear off-balance technique)

You and your opponent face each other in the right middle stance. Your opponent tries to grasp your lapel with his/her right hand. Before your opponent reaches you, with your right knife-hand sweep and push his/her right forearm from the right to the left so that your opponent is forced off-balance to his/her rear.

Practice technique on the opposite side.

b) Aigamae-zenpo-kuzushi (regular stance, front off-balance technique)

You and your opponent face each other in the right middle stance. Your opponent tries to grasp your lapel with his/her right hand. Before your opponent reaches you, with your right knife-hand sweep and push his/her right forearm from the left to the right so that your opponent is forced off-balance to his/her front.

Practice technique on the opposite side.

c) Gyakugamae-koho-kuzushi (reverse stance, rear off-balance technique)

You are in the left foot forward stance; your opponent is in the right foot forward stance and tries to grasp your lapel with his/her right hand. Before your opponent reaches you, with your left knife-hand sweep and push his/her forearm from the right to the left so that your opponent is forced off-balance to his/her rear.

Practice technique on the opposite side.

d) Gyakugamae-zenpo-kuzushi (reverse stance, front off-balance technique)

You are in the left foot forward stance; your opponent is in the right foot forward stance and tries to grasp your lapel with his/her right hand. Before your opponent reaches you, with your left knife-hand sweep and push his/her right forearm from the left to the right so that your opponent is off-balance to his/her front.

Practice technique on the opposite side.

2.   You force your opponent off-balance by pushing and pulling after grasping him/her.

These consist of four ways to upset your opponent's balance: a) Aigamae-koho-kuzushi (regular stance, rear off-balance technique), b) Aigamae-zenpo-kuzushi (regular stance, front off-balance technique), c) Gyakugamae-koho-kuzushi (reverse stance, rear off-balance technique), and d) Gyakugamae-zenpo-kuzushi (reverse stance, front off-balance technique).

a) Aigamae-koho-kuzushi (regular stance, rear off-balance technique)

You and your opponent face each other in the right middle stance. Your opponent tries to grasp your lapel with his/her right hand. Before your opponent reaches you, grasp his/her right wrist from the right with your right hand (the four fingers on top). Push his/her forearm to his/her rear so that your opponent is forced off-balance to his/her rear.

Practice technique on the opposite side.

b) Aigamae-zenpo-kuzushi (regular stance, front off-balance technique)

You and your opponent face each other in the right middle stance. Your opponent tries to grasp your lapel with his/her right hand. Before your opponent reaches you, grasp his/her right wrist from the left with your right hand (the four fingers on top). Push his/her forearm to his/her front so that your opponent is forced off-balance to his/her front.

Practice technique on the opposite side.

c) Gyakugamae-koho-kuzushi (reverse stance, rear off-balance technique)

You are in the left foot forward stance; your opponent is in the right foot forward stance and tries to grasp your lapel with his/her right hand. Before your opponent reaches you, grasp his/her right wrist from the right with your left hand (the four fingers on top). Push his/her forearm to his/her rear so that your opponent is forced off-balance to his/her rear.

Practice technique on the opposite side.

d) Gyakugamae-zenpo-kuzushi (reverse stance, front off-balance technique)

You are in the left foot forward stance; your opponent is in the right foot forward stance and tries to grasp your lapel with his/her right hand. Before your opponent reaches you, grasp your opponent's right elbow from the left with your left hand (the four fingers on top). Push his/her elbow to his/her front so that your opponent is forced off-balance to his/her front.

Practice technique on the opposite side.

I. Practice methods (renshu-ho)

Taking the initiative (sen) is an important skill in Aikido. How do you take the initiative? You do so by discerning the movement of your opponent's attack and by then attacking faster than your opponent. You may perceive some threat from your opponent, for example, the making of a fist. At that time, you must attack more quickly than he or she can. The practice of katas, will facilitate your capacity for "taking the initiative."

Practice methods begin with kata (form) and proceed through randori (free practice) to shiai (contest).

Kata (form) is a restricted and pre-arranged pattern of movement that utilizes both attacking and defending techniques. It is a practical application of the theory of non-resistance. Through practicing kata, you learn how to break your opponent's balance, how to strengthen the postures of your attacks, and how to analyze and apply individual techniques. You need a great deal of form practice because randori is based on kata.

In randori (free practice), you modify and apply the techniques freely in order to develop flexibility. Randori develops strength of endurance and provides actual contest or combat experience.

Shiai (contest) is intended to represent a real fight in which you are involved both emotionally and physically. Mind and body develop through the courage, discipline, self-confidence, and calm needed to prepare for a contest.

J. Solo movement (tandoku-renshu)

This practice prepares you to escape from or counterattack an attacker. It requires an understanding of basic Aikido movement and leads to unbalancing your opponent through such movement, an idea that is fundamental for all the techniques. Your body and hands must work together. In Aikido movements, always open your hand and stretch it in the direction of the movement. All Aikido techniques employ the same basic movements.

There are five ways to practice hand and body movements: 1. Jodan (upper), 2. Chudan (middle), 3. Gedan (lower), 4. Ushiro (rear), and 5. Naname (diagonal).

1. Jodan (upper)

Count 1

You stand in the natural stance. Advance your left foot and then your right foot (tsugi-ashi). Simultaneously stretch your left hand and move it from the lower part of your body upward (palm up) to about face level. Simultaneously, rotate your left hand clockwise, stopping your left hand in front of your face (at this time, the edge of your left knife-hand is directed away from your face). Your right hand is on your right hip. Next, move first your right foot and then your left foot backward (tsugi-ashi) so that you are in your original position. Simultaneously withdraw your left hand behind and above your head (palm up).

Count 2

Advance your left foot and then your right foot (tsugi-ashi). At the same time rotate your left hand and arm counterclockwise, and keep your left hand in front of your face, slightly bending your left arm (palm up). Next, move first your right foot and then your left foot backward (tsugi-ashi), and bring your left hand down to your left side so that you are in your original position.

Count 3

Apply the same movement as in Count 1 except on the opposite side of your body, making the identical moves from your original position.

Count 4

Apply the same movement as in Count 2 except on the opposite side of your body, making the identical moves from your original position.

Chudan (middle)

Count 1

You stand in the natural stance. Advance your left foot and then your right foot (tsugi-ashi); simultaneously, stretch your left hand from your left hip to in front of your chest with a circular motion (palm down). Your right hand is on your right hip. Next, move your right and left foot backward (to the original position), and, at the same time, withdraw your left hand to your left hip (palm up).

Count 2

Advance your left foot and then your right foot (tsugi-ashi), simultaneously stretching your left hand diagonally to the right and then rotate to the left (palm up) so that your left hand is an arm's distance in front of your chest. Next, move first your right foot and then your left foot backward (tsugi-ashi), and bring your left hand back to your left side so that you are in your original position.

Count 3

Apply the same movement as in Count 1 except on the opposite side of your body, making the identical moves from your original position.

Count 4

Apply the same movement as in Count 2 except on the opposite side of your body, making the identical moves from your original position.

3. Gedan (lower)

Count 1

You stand in the natural stance. Advance your left foot, simultaneously raising your right hand up over your head (palm towards you). Next, rotate your right hand down and counterclockwise from above in a circular motion with your right hand near your right knee (at this time, your right palm is down). Turn your body clockwise 180 degrees, and, simultaneously, move your right hand up so that it extends to an arm's length in front of your head (arm extended and palm facing away from your face).

Count 2

Your right hand moves down toward your left knee and clockwise from above in a circular motion with your right hand near your left knee (at this time, your right palm is upwards). Turn your body counterclockwise 180 degrees, and, simultaneously move your right hand up towards you). Move your left foot back, and bring your right hand down to your right side so that you are in your original position.

Count 3

Apply the same movement as in Count 1 except on the opposite side of your body, making the identical moves from your original position.

Count 4

Apply the same movement as in Count 2 except on the opposite side of your body, making the identical moves from your original position.

4. Ushiro (rear)

<u>Count 1</u>

You stand in the natural stance. Your left hand is on your left hip, and your right hand is on your right hip. Advance your left foot forward to a position in front of your right foot. Simultaneously, stretch the fingers of both hands up while raising your right arm toward the ceiling. Turn your body clockwise 180 degrees, and withdraw your right foot backward so that your right foot is next to your left foot. At the same time, return the outstretched right arm to your right hip. (You are now standing opposite your original position.)

Advance your right foot forward to a position in front of your left foot. Simultaneously, stretch the fingers of both hands up while raising your left arm straight toward the ceiling. Turn your body counterclockwise 180 degrees, and withdraw your left foot backward with your left hand down on your left hip while bringing your right hand down to your right hip so that you are in your original position.

Count 3

Apply the same movement as in Count 1 except on the opposite side of your body, making the identical moves from your original position.

Count 4

Apply the same movement as in Count 2 except on the opposite side of your body, making the identical moves from your original position.

5. Naname (diagonal)

Count 1

You stand in the natural stance. Move your right foot backward diagonally to a position just behind your left foot, and step slightly backward diagonally with your left foot; turn your body towards the right. Simultaneously, move your left hand in a circular motion from the left to the right (palm down). Bring your left hand near the right side of your face (at this time, your palm is towards you).

Count 2

Step just a little forward diagonally with your left foot, and step forward diagonally with your right foot. Turn your body to the front so that you are in your original position. Move your left hand forward in circular motion from near the right side of your face to in front of your neck (arm stretched and palm outward).

Count 3

Apply the same movement as in Count 1 except on the opposite side of your body, making the identical moves from your original position.

Count 4

Apply the same movement as in Count 2 except on the opposite side of your body, making the identical moves from your original position.

K. Shuto-awase (knife-hand to knife-hand)

You and your opponent face each other in the right middle stance. Stretch both your right arms forward, keeping them slightly bent. Next, contact each other's right knife-hand in front at neck level. Push against each other's right knife-hand ever so slightly. At this time, both of your left hands rest on your left hips. Now move several steps forward and backward.

Repeat on the opposite side.

Shuto-awase will aid in achieving the proper attack and defense, the regular stance, knife-hand, foot movements, and the development of power (ki) and balance.

V. Techniques

The techniques of Aikido are classified into two different groups: Atemi-waza (the art of attacking the body), and Kansetsu-waza (the art of joint-taking).

Atemi-waza (the art of attacking the body) involves hitting the weak points of your opponent's body with your hand so as to knock out or kill him/her. In Aikido, however, when knocking your opponent off-balance and then pushing or throwing him/her down, it is not necessary to harm him/her.

Kansetsu-waza (the art of joint-taking) involves breaking the joint or causing pain in the opponent's joint, especially his/her wrist and elbow, without causing harm.

In order to develop free practice (randori) in Aikido, and to modernize and systemize the techniques, Professor Kenji Tomiki established a new system called Randori-no-kata (the basic techniques of free practice). Randori-no-kata includes two categories of techniques: 17 Kihon-no-kata (or the 17 basic techniques) and 10 Ura-waza-no-kata (or the 10 counterattacks for kihon-no-kata).

A. KIHON-NO-KATA
(THE 17 BASIC TECHNIQUES)

The 17 basic techniques of Kihon-no-kata are classified into 4 groups: 1. Five atemi-waza (the art of attacking the body), 2. Five hiji-waza (elbow techniques), 3. Four tekubi-waza (wrist techniques), and 4. Three uki-waza (floating techniques).

1. Atemi-waza
(the art of attacking the body)

(1) SHOMEN-ATE
(FRONTAL ATTACK)

You and your opponent approach each other in the right middle stance. When you reach your opponent, you push his/her right forearm away from the inside to the outside with your right knife-hand (shuto).

Then substitute your left hand to keep the opponent's right forearm out of the way. Next, with your right foot step in between your opponent's legs, and with your right palm straight forward on your opponent's chin push upward and advance several steps forward (tsugi-ashi movement) so that your opponent falls down on his/her back.

(2) AIGAMAE-ATE
(REGULAR STANCE ATTACK)

You and your opponent approach each other in the right middle stance. When you reach your opponent, advance your left foot to the outside of his/her right foot, grasp the outside of your opponent's right forearm with both your hands (the four fingers on top), and push it towards the right.

Next, step forward with your right foot to a position behind your opponent's right side; at the same time, extending your right hand through the inside of your opponent's right armpit, push his/her chin with your right palm. Continue to advance in this position several steps forward with tsugi-ashi movement so that your opponent moves

back several steps and then falls down on his/her back.

Variation 1:

   Grasp the outside of his/her right forearm with both your hands, and pull it towards the right side of your hip. Next, step forward with your right foot to a position behind his/her right side. Next, extend your right hand through and above your opponent's right arm, and push his/her chin with your right palm. Then, apply the technique.

(3) GYAKUGAMAE-ATE (REVERSE STANCE ATTACK)

You and your opponent approach each other in the right middle stance. When you reach your opponent, grasp his/her right wrist from the outside with your right hand (the four fingers on top), and pull toward your stomach. Next, step forward with your left foot to a position behind your opponent's right side, and, at the same time, place your left forearm against the upper part of your opponent's chest, pushing him/her backward. Advance several steps with tsugi-ashi movement (toes pointing forward) so that your opponent moves back several steps and then falls down on his/her back.

Variation 1:
    Place your left knife-hand against your opponent's forehead. Then, apply the technique.

Variation 2:
    Place your left forearm against the left side of your opponent's face. Then, apply the technique.

(4). GEDAN-ATE
(LOWER PART ATTACK)

You and your opponent approach each other in the right middle stance. When you reach your opponent, grasp his/her right wrist from the outside with your right hand (the four fingers on top), and pull toward your stomach. Next, step forward with your left foot to behind your opponent's back (toes pointing forward) and, at the same time, pretend you are applying gyakugamae-ate with your left hand.

When, however, your opponent tries to defend himself with his/her left hand, raise up your right hand to in front of your opponent's face. At this moment, push against your opponent's stomach with your left forearm. Advance several steps with tsugi-ashi movement so that your opponent moves back several steps and then falls down on his/her back.

(5) USHIRO-ATE
(BACK ATTACK)

You and your opponent approach each other in the right middle stance. When you reach your opponent, grasp his/her right forearm from the outside with both your hands (the four fingers on top), and push your opponent's forearm towards the left side of his/her chest.

Turn the opponent until you are facing his/her back. Next, advance your right foot to a position behind your opponent's left heel. Then, bring your left foot behind your own right foot, just a little to the left side. At the same time, place both your hands on both of your opponent's shoulders (the four fingers on top), and pull him/her backward so that your opponent falls on his/her back.

2. Hiji-waza (elbow techniques)

(6) OSHI-TAOSHI (PUSH DOWN)

You and your opponent approach each other in the right middle stance. When you reach your opponent, grasp his/her right wrist with your right hand (the four fingers on top), and, at the same time, grasp his/her right forearm with your left hand (the four fingers on top). Withdrawing your left foot diagonally to the left, twist his/her arm clockwise in a circular motion with both your hands.

At this moment, your opponent's right elbow is in front of your face. Next, move your left hand from your opponent's forearm to his/her right elbow, pushing up with your left hand and twisting with your right hand. Immediately, step forward, with first your left foot then your right foot, and push the opponent down on his/her face. After pushing him/her down, hold your opponent's wrist on your right knee, and with your left hand push him/her right elbow.

(7) UDE-GAESHI
(ARM TURN)

You and your opponent approach each other in the right middle stance. When you reach your opponent, grasp his/her right wrist with your right hand (the four fingers on top). At the same time, grasp his/her right forearm with your left hand (the four fingers on top), and try to apply oshi-taoshi. As your opponent bends his/her right elbow to defend against oshi-taoshi, advance your left foot forward to the right side of your opponent.

Next, releasing your left hand, insert your left knife-hand (shuto) from above your opponent's right upper arm, and point your left knife-hand upward. Push opponent's right arm backward with your left knife-hand so that your opponent falls down on his/her back.

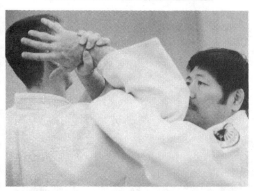

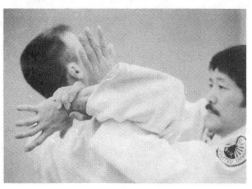

(8) HIKI-TAOSHI
(PULL DOWN)

You and your opponent approach each other in the right middle stance. When you reach your opponent, grasp his/her right wrist with both your hands (the four fingers of the right hand on the upper side of your opponent's wrist, and the four fingers of the left hand on the lower part). Using both your hands, pull your opponent's wrist clockwise and down to your right knee, with your left foot back.

Then, move your right hand from the wrist to the elbow (the four fingers on top), and press your opponent's right elbow from above. Step backward, with first your left foot and then your right foot, and pull your opponent down onto his/her face.

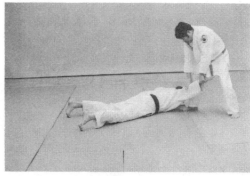

(9) UDE-HINERI (ARM TWIST)

You and your opponent approach each other in the right middle stance. When you reach your opponent, grasp his/her right wrist with both your hands to apply hiki-taoshi. When the opponent resists by pulling and bending his/her right elbow, follow in the direction of this pull with your left foot forward to the right side of his/her back. Release your right hand from your opponent's wrist,

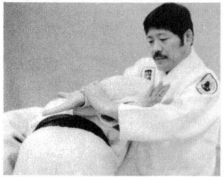

and insert your right knife-hand (shuto) from above his/her right upper arm. Pass your right forearm under your opponent's right armpit, and point your fingers up in front of your face. Twist your opponent's right arm down toward his/her back with your left hand. Turn your body clockwise 180 degrees. Push with your left hand, and pull with your right forearm so that your opponent falls down with the left forward roll (hidari-zenpo-kaiten-ukemi).

(10) WAKI-GATAME
(ARM LOCK)

You and your opponent approach each other in the right middle stance. When you reach your opponent, grasp his/her right wrist with both your hands (left hand from the upper left side, right hand from the lower right side). Stretch out your opponent's right arm, and move your right foot diagonally to the right.

Bring your opponent's right wrist to the right side of your chest with both your hands, holding his/her right elbow under your left armpit. Release your right hand from your opponent's wrist, and put his/her wrist on the inside of your right elbow. Tightly bend your right elbow while securing your opponent's right elbow with your left armpit so that you lock his/her elbow joint.

3. Tekubi-waza
(wrist techniques)

11) KOTE-HINERI
(WRIST TWIST)

You and your opponent approach each other in the right middle stance. When you reach your opponent, grasp his/her right forearm with your left hand, and push it up so that the opponent is off-balance. Next, grasp his/her right four fingers (the back of the hand) from the left side with your right hand. Your right hand twists your opponent's right four fingers clockwise in a circular motion. Next, move your left hand from your opponent's forearm to his/her elbow, pushing the elbow up.

Step forward, with first your left foot then your right foot so that your opponent falls down on his/her face. After this push down, twist your right hand, and push down on your opponent's arm.

(12) KOTE-GAESHI (REVERSE WRIST TWIST)

You and your opponent approach each other in the right middle stance. When you reach your opponent, grasp his/her right forearm with your left hand, and push it up. Next, grasp his/her right four fingers with your right hand, and try to apply kote-hineri. Your opponent, however, resists by bending his/her right elbow. At this time, move your left hand from his/her forearm, and place your left thumb in the middle of the back of your opponent's right hand from the left side, with your four fingers gripped tightly over his/her palm.

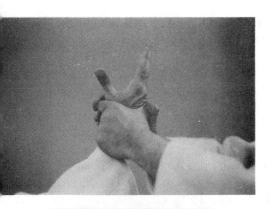

Next, release your right hand from his/her right hand, and place your right thumb likewise in the middle of the back of your opponent's hand from the right side, your four fingers gripped tightly over his/her palm so that your opponent's right hand is gripped by both your hands. Move your left foot backward in a circular motion until it is behind your right foot. At the same time, twist your opponent's wrist counter-clockwise so that your opponent falls down on his/her back.

(13). TENKAI-KOTE-HINERI (ROTATING WRIST TWIST)

You and your opponent approach each other in the right middle stance. When you reach your opponent, push his/her right wrist from the left to the right with your right knife-hand, follow by grasping your opponent's right wrist with your right hand and pull downward in a circle, at the same time, grasp your opponent's right four fingers and the back of the hand from the left side with your left hand. Advance your left foot diagonally to the left, and swing your opponent's hand in a downward clockwise sweep. Next, advance your right foot to your opponent's right side, and pass underneath his/her right armpit, rotating your body counterclockwise 180 degrees.

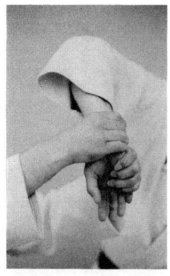

Now with a clockwise twisting motion push your opponent's right elbow upward until it becomes level with his/her face. Advance your right foot forward, and turn your body counterclockwise 180 degrees with your left foot backward. At this time, your opponent's right arm is stretched. Push down on his/her right elbow with your right hand (the four fingers up, inverted V-shape) so that your opponent falls down on his/her face.

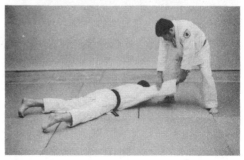

(14) TENKAI-KOTE-GAESHI (ROTATING REVERSE WRIST TWIST)

You and your opponent approach each other in the right middle stance. When you reach your opponent, grasp his/her right wrist with both your hands from the inside (the four fingers of your left hand on the upper part and the four fingers of your right hand on the lower part of your opponent's wrist). Swing your opponent's arm counterclockwise until it is in front of the right side of your face (from the lower part of the circle to the upper part with a twisting motion). Now advance your right foot diagonally to the right, and then advance your left foot diagonally beyond your right foot.

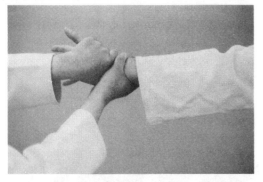

Next, turn your body clockwise 180 degrees, and advance your right foot slightly. At the same time, using both your hands, swing your opponent's right arm (which is on top of your right shoulder) downward in a circle so that your opponent falls down on his/her back.

4. Uki-waza (floating techniques)

(15) MAE-OTOSHI (FRONT DROP)

You and your opponent approach each other in the right middle stance. When you reach your opponent, grasp his/her right wrist with both your hands from the inside (the four fingers of your left hand on the upper part and the four fingers of your right hand on the lower part of your opponent's wrist). Swing your opponent's arm counterclockwise until it is in front of the right side of your face (from the lower part of the circle to the upper part with a twisting motion).

Now advance your left foot diagonally to the right beyond your right foot. At the same time, release your left hand from your opponent's right wrist, and pass your left arm under his/her right armpit with your left hand above your head facing up. Now swing your left hand down from above in a circular motion (palm down) with your left shoulder slightly advanced, pushing on your opponent's right elbow joint so that he/she falls down with the left forward roll (hidari-zenpo-kaiten-ukemi).

(16) SUMI-OTOSHI (CORNER DROP)

You and your opponent approach each other in the right middle stance. When you reach your opponent, grasp his/her right wrist with both your hands from the outside (the four fingers of your right hand on the upper part of your opponent's wrist and the four fingers of your left hand on the lower part of his/her wrist). Twist your opponent's right arm clockwise with both your hands, moving the arm upward from the lower part until it is even with the front of your face. Now advance your left foot diagonally to the left.

Using both your hands, pull his right arm in a circle downward to your left knee so that the opponent falls down on his/her back. After the throw, you should continue to hold your opponent's wrist.

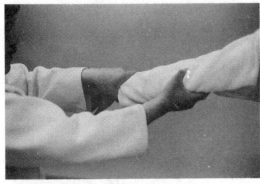

(17) HIKI-OTOSHI (PULL DROP)

You and your opponent approach each other in the right middle stance. When you reach your opponent, move both your feet slightly to the right side, and grasp his/her right wrist with your left hand from the inside (your four fingers up). Immediately grasp your opponent's right elbow with your right hand also from the inside (your thumb up).

Now withdraw your left foot backward, and pull hard with both your hands to the left side of your chest (your left hand twisting his/her wrist counterclockwise as you pull) so that the opponent falls down on his/her back. Next, you turn 180 degrees counterclockwise and continue to hold your opponent's forearm.

B. URA-WAZA-NO-KATA (COUNTERATTACKS FOR KIHON-NO-KATA)

Ura-waza-no-kata consist of 10 techniques. These techniques are classified as: 1. Five atemi-waza-no-ura (counterattacks for atemi-waza), and 2. Five kansetsu-waza-no-ura (counterattacks for kansetsu-waza).

1. Atemi-waza-no-ura (counterattacks for atemi-waza)

(1) SHOMEN-ATE-NO-URA (COUNTERATTACK FOR SHOMEN-ATE)

When your opponent tries to apply shomen-ate but before his/her right hand reaches your chin, withdraw your right foot backward, and grasp your opponent's right wrist with both your hands (palm up). Then, apply right waki-gatame (arm lock).

(2) AIGAMAE-ATE-NO-URA (COUNTERATTACK FOR AIGAMAE-ATE)

When your opponent grasps the outside of your right forearm with both his/her hands and then releases his/her right hand to apply aigamae-ate, withdraw your right foot backward, bend your right arm close to the left side of your chest, and grasp your opponent's left hand with your left hand from above (kote-hineri method).

Next, grasp the back of your opponent's left elbow with your right hand. Advance your right foot, then your left foot, and apply left oshi-taoshi (push down).

(3) GYAKUGAMAE-ATE-NO-URA (COUNTERATTACK FOR GYAKUGAMAE-ATE)

When your opponent tries to apply gyakugamae-ate but before his/her left forearm reaches your upper chest, withdraw your right foot backward, and block his/her left forearm with your left forearm. Simultaneously, pull your right hand out of the grip of his/her right hand.

Now advance your right foot, then apply left gedan-ate (lower part attack).

(4) GEDAN-ATE-NO-URA (COUNTERATTACK FOR GEDAN-ATE)

When your opponent tries to apply gedan-ate but before his/her right hand reaches your stomach, withdraw your right foot backward, and block his/her left forearm with your left forearm (palm down and your left arm stretched toward your opponent's stomach).

Now advance your right foot and your left foot outside his/her left foot; then, apply left aigamae-ate (left regular stance attack).

(5) USHIRO-ATE-NO-URA (COUNTERATTACK FOR USHIRO-ATE)

When your opponent grasps your right forearm with both his/her hands from the outside (the four fingers of both hands on top) and pushes your forearm towards the left side of your chest, you should, simultaneously, advance your left foot and right foot diagonally to the outside of his/her right foot and grasp your opponent's right hand with your left hand (the four fingers on top). then, apply right tenkai-kote-hineri (rotating wrist twist).

2. Kansetsu-waza-no-ura (counterattacks for kansetsu-waza)

(6) OSHI-TAOSHI-NO-URA (COUNTERATTACK FOR OSHI-TAOSHI)

Your opponent grasps your right wrist with his/her right hand (the four fingers on top) and, simultaneously, grasps your right forearm with his/her left hand (the four fingers on top). As your opponent withdraws his/her left foot, advance your right foot, and grasp his/her left hand with your left hand from above (the four fingers on top).

Next, release yourself from his/her right hand, and grasp the back of his/her left elbow with your right hand. Now apply left oshi-taoshi (push down).

(7) HIKI-TAOSHI-NO-URA (COUNTERATTACK FOR HIKI-TAOSHI)

When your opponent grasps your right wrist with both hands (the four fingers of his/her right hand on the upper part and the four fingers of his/her left hand on the lower part of your wrist) and tries to pull your arm down toward his/her right knee, you should, simultaneously, stretch your right fingers toward him/her and grasp your opponent's right hand with your left hand (the thumb on top). Advance first your left foot and then right foot. Now apply right tenkai-kote-hineri (rotating wrist twist).

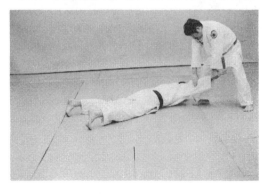

(8) KOTE-GAESHI-NO-URA (COUNTERATTACK FOR KOTE-GAESHI)

When your opponent tries to apply kote-gaeshi but before he/she tries to twist your right wrist, advance your right foot, and grasp the back of your opponent's right hand from the left side with your left hand. Release yourself from his/her grasp, and grasp the back of his/her right hand from the right side with your right hand. Then, apply right kote-gaeshi (reverse wrist twist).

(9) TENKAI-KOTE-HINERI-NO-URA (COUNTERATTACK FOR TENKAI-KOTE-HINERI)

Your opponent grasps your right wrist with both hands, advances first left and then right foot to your right side, and passes under your right armpit, turning counterclockwise 180 degrees. Before your opponent twists your right arm, put your left forearm between your right arm and his/her left arm from underneath. Catch your opponent's left wrist inside your left elbow, and bend your elbow tightly. Now grasp your opponent's left wrist with your right hand, and advance your left foot to your left front corner. Then, apply left waki-gatame (arm lock).

(10) TENKAI-KOTE-GAESHI-NO-URA (COUNTERATTACK FOR TENKAI-KOTE-GAESHI)

Your opponent grasp your right wrist with both hands, pulls down in a circular motion, and advances his/her right foot diagonally to the right; then he/she advances his/her left foot diagonally beyond your right foot. At the same time, you should advance your left foot, then your right foot, diagonally to the outside of his/her left foot, grasping his/her left wrist with your left hand from above (the four fingers on top). Now turn your body counterclockwise 180 degrees. Then, apply left tenkai-kote-gaeshi (rotating reverse wrist twist).

VI. Shichihon-no-kuzushi (the seven off-balance techniques)

Shichihon-no-kuzushi are divided into three classes: A. Kuzushi (off-balance techniques), B. Nage-waza (throwing techniques), and C. Ura-waza (counter-techniques).

A. KUZUSHI (OFF-BALANCE TECHNIQUES)

The kuzushi are divided into 7 groups: 1. Jodan-aigamae (upper regular stance), 2. Jodan-gyakugamae (upper reverse stance), 3. Chudan-aigamae (middle regular stance), 4. Chudan-gyakugamae (middle reverse stance), 5. Gedan-aigamae (lower regular stance), 6. Gedan-gyakugamae (lower reverse stance), and 7. Ushiro ryote-mochi (rear both hands grasp),

1. Jodan-aigamae (upper regular stance)

You and your opponent are in the right foot forward stance. Your opponent grasps your right wrist with his/her right hand. Bend your knees slightly, twist you

Twist your right hand and your body slightly counterclockwise (palm toward you). Now pull slightly to the left until your opponent is standing on his/her toes and is off-balance in the direction of his/her right front corner. (At this time, your right knife-hand is in contact with the inside of your opponent's right wrist.)

2. Jodan-gyakugamae
(upper reverse stance)

You are in the right foot forward stance. Your opponent is in the left foot forward stance. Your opponent grasps your right wrist with his/her left hand. Bend your knees slightly, twist your right hand clockwise (palm up), and bring your right hand straight up above your head. Twist your right hand counterclockwise (palm facing away) and body slightly clockwise and pull slightly to the right until your opponent is standing on his/her toes and is off-balance in the direction of his/her left front corner. (At this time, your right knife-hand is in contact with the inside of the opponent's left wrist.)

3. Chudan-aigamae (middle regular stance)

You and your opponent are in the right foot forward stance. Your opponent grasps your right wrist with his/her right hand. Bend your knees slightly. Bend your right elbow downward from the right to the left simultaneously; move your right hand upward from the left to the right so that your right knife-hand is outside your opponent's right wrist.

Next, advance your left foot diagonally to the left, and twist your body 90 degrees clockwise, pushing your opponent's right wrist with your right knife-hand (perform this at chest level) so that your opponent is off-balance in the direction of his/her left front corner.

4. Chudan-gyakugamae (middle reverse stance)

You are in the right foot forward stance. Your opponent is in the left foot forward stance. Your opponent grasps your right wrist with his/her left hand. Bend your knees slightly. Move your right hand from the left to the outside of your opponent's left wrist, passing your hand under his/her wrist. Bend your right elbow downward; simultaneously, raise your right hand upward, and twist it counterclockwise (palm toward you). Advance your right foot slightly to the outside. Turn your body 90 degrees counterclockwise, and withdraw your left foot to the back of your right foot. (Your right knife-hand is outside your opponent's left wrist.) Push your opponent's left wrist with your right knife-hand (perform this at chest level) so that your opponent is off-balance in the direction of his/her right front corner.

5. Gedan-aigamae
(lower regular stance)

You and your opponent are in the right foot forward stance. Your opponent grasps your right wrist with his/her right hand. Bend your knees slightly, and rotate your right hand from the right to the left in a circle (at this time, your opponent's right palm is facing upward). Now place your right palm on the inside of his/her right wrist. Advance your left foot, and turn your body 90 degrees clockwise. Pull your opponent's right arm downward to your right side so that your opponent is off-balance in the direction of his/her front.

6. Gedan-gyakugamae (lower reverse stance)

You are in the right foot forward stance. Your opponent is in the left foot forward stance. Your opponent grasps your right wrist with his/her left hand. Bend your knees slightly. Bend your right wrist toward you (palm inward). Withdraw your left foot to the back of your right foot, while turning your body 90 degrees counter-clockwise. Pull your right wrist to the front of your stomach, rotating your right palm clockwise until your right palm is up. Your opponent's left arm follows your right arm (his/her palm up) so that your opponent is off-balance in the direction of his/her front.

7. Ushiro-ryote-mochi
(rear both hands grasp)

You and your opponent are in the right foot forward stance. Your opponent grasps your right wrist with his/her right hand (the four fingers up). Now your opponent moves his/her left foot around and steps behind you, while he/she grasps your left hand with his/her left hand (the four fingers up).

Bend your knees. Advance your left foot to a position in front of your right foot, and point your toes to the right. Simultaneously, raise your right hand straight upward to the right side above your head. Stretch your left fingers upward, and move your hand forward slightly around your left hip. Now turn your body 90 degrees clockwise so that your opponent is off-balance in the direction of his/her left front corner.

B. NAGE-WAZA (THROWING TECHNIQUES)

Nage-waza (the throwing techniques) are divided into 7 groups: 1. Jodan aigamae-nage-waza (upper regular stance throwing technique), 2. Jodan-gyakugamae nage-waza (upper reverse stance throwing technique), 3. Chudan-aigamae-nage-waza (middle regular stance throwing technique), 4. Chudan-gyakugamae-nage-waza (middle reverse stance throwing technique), 5. Gedan-aigamae-nage-waza (lower regular stance throwing technique), 6. Gedan-gyakugamae-nage-waza (lower reverse stance throwing technique), and 7. Ushiro-ryote-mochi-nage-waza (rear both hand grasp throwing technique).

1. Jodan-aigamae-nage-waza (upper regular stance throwing technique)

Apply the same movement as jodan-aigamae up to the point where your opponent is off-balance. Next, pivoting on your right foot to the left, move your left foot behind it. At the same time, turn your body counterclockwise, and move several steps (right foot forward) in a circle while pulling your opponent's right hand with your knife-hand (perform this above your head) so that your opponent moves around your right side on the tip of his/her toes. Now pull and push your opponent's right wrist with your right knife-hand so that your opponent falls into the right forward roll.

2. Jodan-gyakugamae-nage-waza (upper reverse stance throwing technique)

Apply the same movement as jodan-gyakugamae up to the point where your opponent is off-balance. next, pivoting on your right foot to the right, move your left foot behind it. Simultaneously, turn your body clockwise, and move several steps (the right foot forward) in a circle while pulling his/her left wrist with your right knife-hand (perform this above your head) so that your opponent moves around your left side on the tip of his/her toes. Now pull and push your opponent's left wrist with your right knife-hand so that Your opponent falls into the left forward roll.

3. Chudan-aigamae-nage-waza (middle regular stance throwing technique)

Apply the same movement as chudan-aigamae up to the point where your opponent is off-balance. Move yourself several steps (the right foot forward) in a circle, pushing his/her right wrist with your right knife-hand (perform this at chest level) so that your opponent moves around your left side on the tip of his/her toes. Push your opponent's right wrist forward with your right knife-hand. Your opponent then falls into the left forward roll.

4. Chudan-gyakugamae-nage waza (middle reverse stance throwing technique)

Apply the same movement as chudan-gyakugamae up to the point where your opponent is off-balance. Move yourself several steps (the right foot forward) in a circle, pushing his/her left wrist with your right knife-hand (perform this at chest level) so that your opponent moves around your right side on the tip of his/her toes. Push your opponent's left wrist forward with your right knife-hand. Your opponent then falls into the right forward roll.

5. Gedan-aigamae-nage-waza (lower regular stance throwing technique)

Apply the same movement as gedan-aigamae up to the point where your opponent is off-balance. Move yourself several steps (the right foot forward) in a circle, pulling his/her right wrist with your right palm (perform this at upper right leg level) so that your opponent moves around your left side on the tips of his/her toes. Next, with your right hand, pull his/her right wrist upward until it is positioned an arm's length in front of your head (arm extended and palm away from you). Your opponent moves several steps forward past you and falls down on his/her back.

6. Gedan-gyakugamae-nage-waza (lower reverse stance throwing technique)

Apply the same movement as gedan-gyakugamae up to the point where your opponent is off-balance. Move yourself several steps (the right foot forward) in a circle, pulling his/her left hand with your right wrist (perform this at upper right leg level) so that your opponent move around your right side on the tip of his/her toes. Next, with your right hand, pull his/her right wrist upward until it is positioned an arm's length in front of your head (arm extended and palm towards you). Your opponent moves several steps forward past you and falls down on his/her back.

7. Ushiro-ryote-mochi-nage-waza (rear both hands grasp throwing technique)

Apply the same movement as ushiro-ryote-mochi up to the point where your opponent is off-balance. At the same time, turn your body 90 degrees clockwise so that your opponent falls down into the left forward roll.

C. URA-WAZA (COUNTERTECHNIQUES)

The ura-waza are divided into 7 groups: 1. Jodan-aigamae-ura-waza (upper regular stance countertechnique), 2. Jodan-gyakugamae-ura-waza (upper reverse stance countertechnique), 3. Chudan-aigamae-ura-waza (middle regular stance countertechnique), 4. Chudan-gyakugamae-ura-waza (middle reverse stance countertechnique), 5. Gedan-aigamae-ura-waza (lower regular stance countertechnique), 6. Gedan-gyakugamae-ura-waza (lower reverse stance countertechnique), and 7. Ushiro-ryote-mochi-ura-waza (rear both hands grasp countertechnique).

1. Jodan-aigamae-ura-waza (upper regular stance countertechnique)

You apply the same movement as jodan-aigamae-nage-waza, but your opponent resists your throwing technique.

In response, with your right knife-hand, push down your opponent's right wrist counterclockwise in a circle to in front of your navel. Then, with the same hand, grasp his/her right wrist from above (the four fingers on top),

and bring his/her right hand up from the lower part of the circle to the upper part with a twisting motion. Next, with your left hand, grasp your opponent's right elbow from the outside (the thumb on top). Advance your right foot, and, simultaneously, push his/her right elbow forward as you push his/her right wrist downward in a circle so that your opponent falls into a left forward roll.

2. Jodan-gyakugamae-ura-waza (upper reverse stance countertechnique)

You apply the same movement as jodan-gyakugamae-nage-waza, but your opponent resists your throwing technique. In response, with your right knife-hand, push down your opponent's left wrist clockwise in a circle until his/her right hand is in front of your navel. With your right hand, grasp his/her left wrist from above (the thumb on top),

and bring his/her left hand from the lower part of the circle to the upper part with a twisting motion. Next, with your left hand, grasp your opponent's left wrist from above (the four fingers on top). Release your right hand from his/her left wrist, and employ it to his/her left elbow from the outside (the thumb on top). Now advance your left foot and, simultaneously, push his/her left elbow forward as you push his/her left wrist downward so that your opponent falls into a right forward roll.

3. Chudan-aigamae-ura-waza (middle regular stance countertechnique)

You apply the same movement as chudan-aigamae-nage-waza, but your opponent resists your throwing technique. In response, with your right hand, grasp your opponent's right wrist from the outside (the four fingers on top), and, with your left hand, grasp his/her right elbow from the outside (the four fingers on top). Next, release your right hand from his/her right hand. Turn your body counterclockwise 180 degrees, and bring your right upper arm to the front of his/her neck;

now advance your right foot so that your opponent falls down onto his/her back.

4. Chudan-gyakugamae-ura-waza (middle reverse stance countertechnique)

You apply the same movement as chudan-gyakugamae-nagewaza, but your opponent resists your throwing technique. In response, with your right hand, grasp your opponent's left wrist (the four fingers on top), and, with your left hand, grasp his/her left hand from below (the thumb toward you).

Next, release your right hand from his/her left wrist, and apply left gyakugamae-ate so that your opponent falls down onto his/her back.

5. Gedan-aigamae-ura-waza (lower regular stance countertechnique)

You apply the same movement as gedan-aigamae-nage-waza, but your opponent resists your throwing technique. In response, turn your body 180 degrees counterclockwise, and advance your right foot to a position behind your opponent's right foot.

Next, bring the inside of your right elbow to your opponent's face, and push it so that your opponent falls down on his/her back.

6. Gedan-gyakugamae-ura-waza (lower reverse stance countertechnique)

You apply the same movement as gedan-gyakugamae-nage-waza, but your opponent resists your throwing technique. In response, turn your body 180 degrees clockwise. Bring the back of your right hand to his/her face (drawing it in a circle from the lower part to the upper part, palm up).

Simultaneously, advance your right foot to a position behind your opponent's left foot. Apply left gyakugamae-ate.

7. Ushiro-ryote-mochi-ura-waza (rear both hands grasp countertechnique)

Apply the same movement as ushiro-ryote-mochi-nage-waza, but your opponent resists your throwing technique. In response, advance your right foot to the outside of your opponent's right foot, and bring your right hand to a position slightly in front of the top of your head. Turn your body 90 degrees counterclockwise;

at this time, bring your right hand down to near your left thigh so that you pass just underneath his/her right armpit and your left upper arm is in contact with his/her right elbow. Advance your left foot, and apply right mae-otoshi.

VII. Tanto-ni-taisuru Kihon-no-kata (the knife techniques corresponding to the 17 basic techniques).

The knife techniques corresponding to the 17 basic techniques are the same as the 17 basic techniques themselves except that your opponent has a knife in his/her right hand and thrusts it at you. Also your body movements are slightly different. I will explain here how to apply the techniques in this situation.

You and your opponent are facing each other at a reaching distance when your opponent advances one step. You are in the right foot forward stance, and your right shuto (knife-hand) is placed in front of your lower abdomen (right lower stance).

Your opponent is also in the right foot forward stance and holds a knife in his/her right hand (knife-blade on top). Your opponent's knife is placed in front of his/her lower abdomen (right lower knife stance). Your opponent advances his/her right foot and thrusts the knife straight at your solar plexus. The knife techniques of the 17 basic techniques always begin with the abovementioned stances.

1. Shomen-ate

Your opponent advances his/her right foot and thrusts a knife straight at your solar plexus. Before your opponent's knife reaches you, turn your body slightly counter-clockwise. Simultaneously, move your left foot to a position behind your right foot. Block your opponent's right forearm with your right knife-hand. Then, substitute your left hand to keep the opponent's right forearm out of the way. Advance your right foot then left foot; apply shomen-ate.

2. Aigamae-ate

Your opponent advances his/her right foot and thrusts a knife straight at your solar plexus. Before your opponent's knife reaches you, advance your left foot diagonally to the left; at the same time, turn your body clockwise 90 degrees. Grasp your opponent's right forearm with both your hands (the four fingers on top). Turn your body counterclockwise 90 degrees, and step forward with your right foot to a position behind your opponent's right side. Next, apply aigamae-ate.

3. Gyakugamae-ate

Your opponent advances his/her right foot and thrusts a knife straight at your solar plexus. Before your opponent's knife reaches you, move your left foot and body to the left. Next, grasp his/her right wrist with your right hand from the left (the four fingers on top). Advance your left foot to a position behind your opponent's right foot. Bring his/her right wrist toward the right side of your hip. Place the outside of your left upper arm against the upper part of your opponent's chest, and apply gyakugamae-ate.

4. Gedan-ate

Your opponent advances his/her right foot and thrusts a knife straight at your solar plexus. Before your opponent's knife reaches you, move your left foot and body to the left. Next, grasp his/her right wrist with your right hand from the left (the four fingers on top). Raise your left hand, and pretend you are applying gyakugamae-ate with your left hand so that your opponent tries to defend himself/herself with his/her left hand. Next, raise your opponent's right wrist up above your head with your right hand. Advance your left foot to a position far behind your opponent's right foot. At the same time, push against your opponent's stomach with the outside of your left upper arm (at this time, your left shoulder should be lower than his/her chest, the left side of your body should contact the front of his/her body, and the front of your upper leg should contact the back of his/her upper leg). Push your opponent's stomach with your left arm and body so that your opponent falls down on his/her back.

5. Ushiro-ate

Your opponent advances his/her right foot and thrusts a knife straight at your solar plexus. Before your opponent's knife reaches you, move your body and left foot to the left, and turn your body slightly clockwise. At the same time, grasp your opponent's right elbow with your left hand and his/her right wrist with your right hand (the four fingers on top). Pull your opponent's right arm toward the right side of your body with both your hands so that your opponent is forced off-balance to his/her front. Next, advance your right foot to a position behind your opponent's left heel. Bring your left foot behind your own right foot, just a little to the left side. Place both your hands on both of your opponent's shoulders, and apply ushiro-ate.

6. Oshi-taoshi

Your opponent advances his/her right foot and thrusts a knife straight at your solar plexus. Before your opponent's knife reaches you, withdraw your left foot diagonally to the left, and turn your body clockwise 45 degrees. Grasp his/her right wrist with your right hand; simultaneously, grasp his/her right forearm with your left hand. Next, apply oshi-taoshi.

7. Ude-gaeshi

Your opponent advances his/her right foot and thrusts a knife straight at your solar plexus. Before your opponent's knife reaches you, withdraw your left foot diagonally to the left, and turn your body clockwise 45 degrees. Grasp his/her right wrist with your right hand. At the same time, grasp his/her forearm with your left hand. You apply oshi-taoshi, but your opponent rejects it, so that you apply ude-gaeshi.

8. Hiki-taoshi

Your opponent advances his/her right foot and thrusts a knife straight at your solar plexus. Before your opponent's knife reaches you, withdraw your left foot diagonally to the left, and turn your body clockwise 45 degrees. Next, grasp your opponent's right wrist from the left with both your hands; then, apply hiki-taoshi.

9. Ude-hineri

Your opponent advances his/her right foot and thrusts a knife straight at your solar plexus. Before your opponent's knife reaches you, withdraw your left foot diagonally to the left, and turn your body clockwise 45 degrees. Grasp your opponent's right wrist from the left with both your hands. You apply hikitaoshi, but he/she rejects by pulling his/her arm. At this moment, you apply ude-hineri.

10. Waki-gatame

Your opponent advances his/her right foot and thrusts a knife straight at your solar plexus. Before your opponent's knife reaches you, withdraw your right foot to a position behind your left foot, and turn your body clockwise 90 degrees. Grasp his/her right wrist from the left with both your hands. Next, apply waki-gatame.

11. Kote-hineri

Your opponent advances his/her right foot and thrusts a knife straight at your solar plexus. Before your opponent's knife reaches you, withdraw your left foot diagonally to the left, and turn your body clockwise 45 degrees. Grasp his/her right forearm with your left hand, And, grasp his/her right hand from the left side with your right hand. Then, apply kote-hineri.

12. Kote-gaeshi

Your opponent advances his/her right foot and thrusts a knife straight at your solar plexus. Before your opponent's knife reaches you, withdraw your left foot diagonally to the left, and turn your body clockwise 45 degrees. Grasp his/her right hand from above with your left hand, and grasp his/her right hand from underneath with your right hand., Then, apply kote-gaeshi.

13. Tenkai-kote-hineri

Your opponent advances his/her right foot and thrusts a knife straight at your solar plexus. Before your opponent's knife reaches you, move your body and left foot to the left, and turn your body clockwise slightly. And grasp his/her right hand with both your hands from the outside. Next, apply tenkai-kote-hineri.

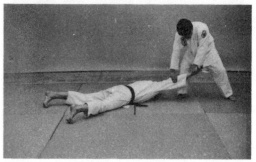

14. Tenkai-kote-gaeshi

Your opponent advances his/her right foot and thrusts a knife straight at your solar plexus. Before your opponent's knife reaches you, move your body and left foot to the right, and turn your body counterclockwise slightly. Grasp your opponent's right hand with both your hands from the inside Next, apply tenkai-kote-gaeshi.

15. Mae-otoshi

Your opponent advances his/her right foot and thrusts a knife straight at your solar plexus. Before your opponent's knife reaches you, move your body and left foot to the right, and turn your body counterclockwise slightly. Grasp his/her right wrist with both your hands from the inside. Advance your right foot diagonally to the right. Next, advance your left foot between your right foot and his/her right foot. Then apply mae-otoshi.

16. Sumi-otoshi

Your opponent advances his/her right foot and thrusts a knife straight at your solar plexus. Before your opponent's knife reaches you, move your body and left foot to the left, and turn your body clockwise 45 degrees. Grasp his/her right wrist with both your hands from the outside. Then, apply sumi-otoshi.

17. Hiki-otoshi

Your opponent advances his/her right foot and thrusts a knife straight at your solar plexus. Before your opponent's knife reaches you, withdraw your right foot diagonally to the right, and turn your body counterclockwise slightly. Grasp his/her right wrist with your left hand from the inside and right elbow with your right hand from the inside. Withdraw your left foot, and apply hiki-otoshi.

VIII. Suwari-waza (kneeling techniques)

The tradition in old Japan was that Japanese people would customarily perform a kneeling bow for courtesy to others when in their home. The following kneeling techniques were used where an enemy attacks suddenly from a kneeling position. Presently, the same techniques are practiced in aikido and other martial arts forms.

Here I present forms, from the beginning through the advanced techniques.

Before you start kneeling techniques, you should practice Shikko (kneeling walk) because kneeling walk and kneeling techniques are working with harmonious movements

SHIKKO (kneeling walk)

From kneeling position, move your upper body up and advance your left foot forward (knee up). At the same time, move your right foot behind your left foot. Next, put your left knee on the ground and advance your right foot forward (knee up).

Simultaneously, draw your left foot back toward your right foot. Then repeat on the opposite side.

1. Ryote-mochi-naname-nage
(both hands grasp, diagonal throw)

Your opponent grasps both your wrists with both his/her hands. Bend both your elbows down. At the same time, rotate your fingertips up. Push the inside of his/her right wrist with your left knife-hand toward his/her right rear downward.

Simultaneously stretch your right knife-hand up toward your opponent's chest so that your opponent falls down in front of your left front corner. Now advance your left foot diagonally to the left then your right foot. Next, place the inside of his/her wrists to the mat with your left knife-hand, and push your opponent's chest with your right knife-hand so that you can control him/her. Your opponent maintains his/her grasp continuously throughout the throw.

2. Ude-mochi-tekubi-kime (one-arm grasp, wrist lock)

Your opponent grasps the left side of your upper arm with his/her right hand. Hold your opponent's right hand tightly against your upper arm with your right hand. Bring your left arm up from the left to the right with a circular motion so that your left arm is above his/her right wrist.

At this moment, his/her right knife-hand is facing up. Next move your body backward slightly and turn your body a little to the right, and push down on the knife-hand side of his/her right wrist with your left arm so that you can take your opponent's right wrist joint.

3. Ude-mochi-hiji-kime
(one-arm grasp, elbow lock)

Your opponent grasps the left side of your upper arm with his/her right hand. Hold your opponent's right hand tightly with your right hand. Bring your left arm to the back of your opponent's right elbow.

Move your body backward slightly and turn your body a little to the right, and push down on the back of your opponent's right elbow with your left knife-hand so that you lock his/her right elbow.

4. Eri-mochi-kote-hineri
(collar grasp, wrist twist)

Your opponent grasps your right collar with his/her right hand. Withdraw your right foot. Grasp your opponent's right hand from above, and twist it clockwise with your right hand (kote-hineri) so that you can release his/her hold. Push his/her right elbow with your left hand until your opponent's stomach touches on the mat. Next, hold his/her arm against the mat with both your hands.

5. Katate-mochi-ude-hineri (one-hand grasp, arm twist)

Your opponent grasps your left wrist with his/her right hand. Hold your opponent's right hand tightly against your left wrist with your right hand. Bring your left hand up above his/her wrist from the outside (now your opponent's right wrist is in front of your chest). Your opponent does not release his/her grasping hand from your left wrist. Next, push down the knife-hand side of his/her right wrist with your left knife-hand so that your opponent goes down to the mat.

Next, bring his/her right wrist between your left upper arm and left forearm with your right hand. Then, hold it tightly with your left forearm and left upper arm. Release your right hand from his/her right hand. Bring your right knife hand to the back of his/her right elbow. Press his/her right elbow downward with your right knife-hand. At the same time, push his/her right wrist forward with your left arm so that you can twist his/her arm and lock it.

6. Ryote-hidarite-mochi-ushiro-taoshi
(two hands on the left wrist grasp, rear throw)

Your opponent grasps your left wrist with both his/her hands. Move your left hand from the left to the right, and bring upward in a circular motion until your left knife-hand is in front of your face (knife-hand outward).

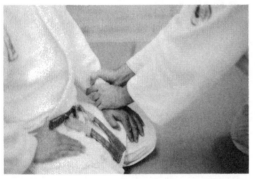

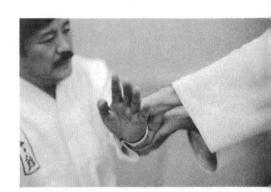

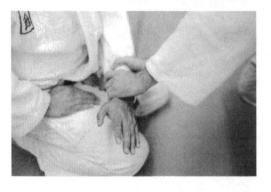

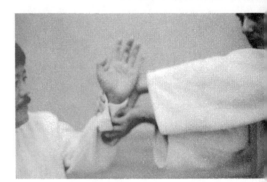

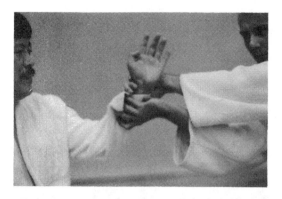

Next support your left hand with your open right hand. Then, stretch your knife-hand toward your opponent's face so that your opponent falls down on his/her back.

7. Ryote-mochi-waki-gatame
(both hands grasp, arm lock)

Your opponent grasps both your wrists with both his/her hands. Pull both your hands backward to your sides, and at the same time, bring your upper body up. Then, kick your opponent's groin with your right knee. Withdraw your right foot backward (at this time, both of your knees and balls of the foot are on the mat).

Release your right wrist from his/her left hand by pulling to the left. Next, grasp his/her right wrist with both your hands. With a twisting motion, bring his/her wrist to your right chest. At the same time, turn your body 90 degrees clockwise, and apply waki-gatame.

8. Migite-hidarite-mochi-te-kime (right hand on the left wrist grasp, hand lock)

Your opponent grasps your left wrist with his/her right hand. Move your left hand from the left to the right. With continuous motion, rotate your left hand counterclockwise (palm up). At this moment, your opponent holds tightly to your left wrist (palm up). Put down your left elbow and upper body, and press his/her right hand down so that you can lock his/her right wrist.

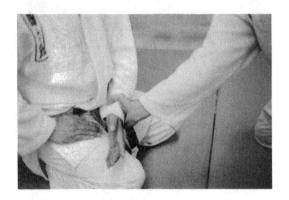

9. Ryote-mochi-yoko-nage
(both hands grasp, side throw)

Your opponent grasps both your hands with both his/her hands. Bend both your elbows down, and fingertips up.

Push the inside of his/her right wrist with your left knife-hand out from your left side (fingertips toward your left), and simultaneously stretch your right arm toward your left side (fingertips toward your left) so that your opponent falls down on his/her back. (Roll sideways, do not stand.)

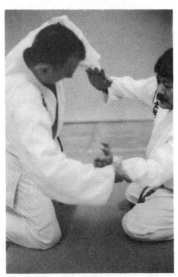

10. Ryote-mochi-ushiro-nage
(both hands grasp, rear throw)

Your opponent grasps both your wrists with both his/her hands. Bend both your wrists downward with palm down. Next, bend both your elbows down. At the same time, bring your wrists upward so that your opponent stands up.

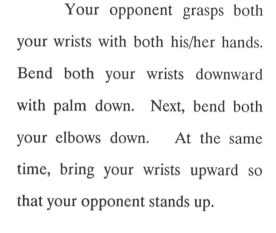

With a continuous motion, pull your wrists backward. (Your left wrist should pull slightly harder than your right wrist.) Your opponent advances his/her right foot and applies right zenpo-kaiten-ukemi.

XI. Aiki-goshin-ho
(aiki self-defense method)

There are many crimes going on in the world. One needs to protect oneself from crimes. The philosophy of aikido is not to harm your opponent, but sometimes, one can not avoid an attacker. There are many different attacking patterns such as strikes, thrusts, and kicks, etc. I have explained the self-defense techniques that follow.

1. Shomen-uchi (head strike)

2. Yokomen-uchi (side face strike)

3. Chudan-tsuki (middle thrust)

4. Jodan-tsuki (upper thrust)

5. Mae-geri (front kick)

6. Mawashi-geri (round kick)

7. Yoko-geri (side kick)

8. Ushiro-geri (rear kick)

1. Shomen-uchi (head strike)

You and your opponent face each other in the left middle stance. Your opponent advances his/her right foot and strikes the top of your head from above with the fist edge of his/her right fist. Before your opponent's fist reaches you, withdraw your left foot diagonally to the left. Grasp his/her right wrist with your right hand (the four fingers on top). Simultaneously, grasp his/her right elbow with your left hand (the four fingers on top). Next, apply oshi-taoshi (push down).

2. Yokomen-uchi
   (side face strike)

You and your opponent face each other in the left middle stance. Your opponent advances his/her right foot and strikes the left side of your face with his/her right knife-hand (shuto) (the palm side up).

Advance your right foot diagonally to the right, and grasp his/her right wrist from the inside with your left hand (the four fingers on top). At the same time, grasp his/her right wrist with your right hand (the thumb on top) (your hands are facing each other on either side of your opponent's wrist). Advance your left foot diagonally to the right and apply tenkai-kote-gaeshi.

3. Chudan-tsuki (middle thrust)

You and your opponent face each other in the left middle stance. Your opponent advances his/her right foot and thrusts his/her right fist toward your solar plexus. Withdraw your right foot diagonally to the left so that you can avoid his/her thrusting fist. Next, grasp your opponent's right hand from above with your left hand (the four fingers on top), and grasp his/her right hand from below with your right hand (the thumb on top).

Withdraw your left foot diagonally to the left and apply kote-gaeshi.

4. Jodan-tsuki
(upper thrust)

You and your opponent face each other in the left middle stance. Your opponent advances his/her right foot and thrusts his/her right fist toward your face. Push away your opponent's right forearm with your left hand.

At the same time, turn your body 90 degrees to the right and withdraw your right foot diagonally to the left passing your left foot. Then turn your body 180 degrees to the left. Strike the back of his/her neck with your right elbow. Advance your left foot diagonally to the right and turn your body 90 degrees to the left so that you are now behind your opponent's left side and apply ushiro-ate.

5. Mae-geri (front kick)

You and your opponent face each other in the left middle stance. Your opponent advances his/her right foot and kicks your groin with his/her right foot. Advance your right foot diagonally to the right and with your left forearm push away his/her right foot to the left. Next, apply right shomen-ate.

6. Mawashi-geri (round kick)

You and your opponent face each other in the left middle stance. Your opponent advances his/her right foot and kicks the left side of your face with his/her right foot. Advance your right foot diagonally to the right to avoid his/her kick. Grasps his/her right foot from above with both your hands (the four fingers on top). Then, bring it to your left armpit.

Advance your right foot between your opponent's feet passing the leg, and sweep his/her left leg from the left to the right with the back of your right leg so that your opponent falls down on his/her back.

7. Yoko-geri (side kick)

You and your opponent face each other in the left middle stance. Your opponent kicks your stomach with his/her right side kick. Advance your left foot diagonally to the left and with your right forearm push away his/her right foot to the right. Bring your left upper arm in front of your opponent's neck and apply gyakugamae-ate.

8. Ushiro-geri (back kick)

You and your opponent face each other in the left middle stance. Your opponent turns his/her body 180 degrees to the right and applies right back kick to your stomach. Advance your left foot diagonally to the left. Therefore, you can avoid his/her kick. Grasp and pull down your opponent's face from the front with your left hand. At the same time, bend your knees, and sweep the back of his/her left leg with your right arm so that your opponent falls backward.

X. PROMOTION REQUIREMENTS

These are the basic promotion requirements for the United States Tomiki Aikido Association: You must have good moral character, attitude, maturity, skill proficiency, knowledge, experience, contribution, and time in grade. The applicant must demonstrate the seii (sincerity, faith and trust), kinro (labor, endeavor, and exertion), kenshiki (knowledge, insight, dignity and awareness), and kihaku (spirit) in the classes, during the test, as well as proficiency in activities. Promotion tests are conducted by a combination of oral and skill demonstration, and written examination. There are two candidate classifications: 1. Shiai players (competitors), 2. Nonshiai players (noncompetitors).

1. Shiai players

> Shiai players mean active competitors. Instructors are considered shiai players. All shiai points must be received from the Unites States Tomiki Aikido Association sanctioned shiai. The point system is as follows: If you win by Ippon (full point), you receive one point. If you win by Waza-ari (half point), you receive a half point. If you win by Yusei-gachi (decision), you receive a quarter point. Shiai points are counted for one promotion so that you need new points to be promoted to the next rank.

2. Nonshiai players

Nonshiai players mean noncompetitors, these students never attended the shiai but always practice Aikido and contribute to the art. Students who do not compete in shiai will be obligated to attend double the amount of class time in order to receive their promotion test.

From White Belt to 8th kyu - Yellow belt

Time in grade: Minimum of three months practice (twice a week)

Shiai points: 1 (tournament experience)

Promotion test score: An average of 5

Philosophy of Aikido:
What is Aikido? 1
History of Aikido 5
The Values of Aikido 10

Basic Knowledge:
The Bow (rei) 11
Breakfall (ukemi) 14
The Distance (maai) 23
Eye Contact (metsuke) 25
The Knife-hand (shuto) 26
The Stances (kamae) 27
Foot Movement (unsoku) 29
Off-balance Techniques (kuzushi) 35
Practice Methods (renshu-ho) 41
Solo Movement (tandoku-renshu) 42

Kihon-no-kata (the 17 basic techniques)
(1) Shomen-ate (frontal attack) 56
(2) Aigamae-ate (regular stance attack) 58
(3) Gyakugamae-ate (reverse stance attack) 60
(4) Gedan-ate (lower part attack) 62
(5) Ushiro-ate (back attack) 64

Suwari-waza (kneeling techniques)
(1) Ryote-mochi-naname-nage (both hands grasp, diagonal throw) 163
(2) Ude-mochi-tekubi-kime (one-arm grasp, wrist lock) 165
(3) Ude-mochi-hiji-kime (one-arm grasp, elbow lock) 167

Variation of Shomen-ate
   (1) Tekubi-tori
   (2) Mae-eri-tori
   (3) Juji-jime

From 8th kyu to 7th kyu - Yellow Belt and Red Stripe

Time in grade: Minimum of three months practice (twice a week)

Shiai points: 2

Promotion test score: An average of 5.5

Kihon-no-kata (the 17 basic techniques)
   (6) Oshi-taoshi (push down) 66
   (7) Ude-gaeshi (arm turn) 68
   (8) Hiki-taoshi (pull down) 70

Suwari-waza (kneeling techniques)
   (4) Eri-mochi-kote-hineri (collar grasp, wrist twist) 169
   (5) Katate-mochi-ude-hineri (one-hand grasp, arm twist) 170

Variation of Gyakugamae-ate
   (1) Tekubi-tori
   (2) Sode-tori-1
   (3) Sode-tori-2

One arm against one hands
   (1) Nigiri-oshi-nage
   (2) Ude-hineri-nage
   (3) Ude-gaeshi-nage

Basic techniques
   (1) Katate-tori-shiho-nage
   (2) Katate-tori-kote-gaeshi

From 7th kyu to 6th kyu - Green Belt

Time in grade: Minimum of three months practice (twice a week)

Shiai points: 3

Promotion test score: An average of 6

Kihon-no-kata (the basic techniques)
    (9) Ude-hineri (arm twist) 72
    (10) Waki-gatame (arm lock) 74
    (11) Kote-hineri (wrist twist) 76

Suwari-waza (kneeling techniques)
    (6) Ryote-hidarite-mochi-ushiro-taoshi (two hands on one wrist grasp, rear throw) 172
    (7) Ryote-mochi-waki-gatame (both hands grasp, arm lock) 174

Variation of Gyakugamae-ate
    (4) Sode-tori-3
    (5) Ryo-sode-tori
    (6) Ushiro-eri-tori

From 6th kyu to 5th kyu - Green Belt and Red Stripe

Time in grade: Minimum of three months practice (twice a week)

Shiai points: 4

Promotion test score: An average of 6.5

Kihon-no-kata (the 17 basic techniques)
    (12) Kote-gaeshi (reverse wrist twist) 78
    (13) Tenkai-kote-hineri (rotating wrist twist) 80
    (14) Tenkai-kote-gaeshi (rotating reverse wrist twist) 82

Suwari-waza (kneeling techniques)
    (8) Migite-hidarite-mochi-te-kime (right hand on left wrist grasp, hand lock) 176

Variation of Aigamae-ate
    (1) Te-kubi-tori
    (2) Mae-eri-tori

Shichihon-no-kuzushi (the seven off-balance techniques)
    Kuzushi (off-balance techniques)
        (1) Jodan-aigamae (upper regular stance) 110
        (2) Jodan-gyakugamae (upper reverse stance) 112
        (3) Chudan-aigamae (middle regular stance) 113
        (4) Chudan-gyakugamae (middle reverse stance) 114
        (5) Gedan-aigamae (lower regular stance) 116
        (6) Gedan-gyakugamae (lower reverse stance) 117
        (7) Ushiro-ryote-mochi (rear both hands grasp) 118

Basic techniques
    (3) Ryote-tori-shiho-nage
    (4) Ryote-tori-kote-gaeshi-ude-hineri

From 5th kyu to 4th kyu - Purple Belt

Time in grade: Minimum of three months practice (twice a week)

Shiai-points: 5
Promotion test score: An average of 7

Kihon-no-kata (the 17 basic techniques)
    (15) Mae-otoshi (front drop) 84
    (16) Sumi-otoshi (corner drop) 86

Suwari-waza (kneeling techniques)
    (9) Ryote-mochi-yoko-nage (both hands grasp, side throw) 177

Variation of Oshi-taoshi
    Tekubi-tori

From 4th kyu to 3rd kyu - Purple Belt and Red Stripe

Time in grade: Minimum of three months practice (twice a week)

Shiai points: 6

Promotion test score: An average of 7.5

Kihon-no-kata (the 17 basic techniques)
    (17) Hiki-otoshi (pull drop) 88

Suwari-waza (kneeling techniques)
    (10) Ryote-mochi-ushiro-nage (both hands grasp, rear throw) 179

Variation of Hiki-taoshi
    Tekubi-tori

One arm against both hands
    (1) Suihei-mawaashi
    (2) Ude-hineri-nage
    (3) Ude-gaeshi-nage

Basic techniques
    (5) Yokomen-uchi-shiho-nage
    (6) Shomen-uchi-shiho-nage

From 3rd kyu to 2nd kyu - Brown Belt

Time in grade: Minimum of three months practice (twice a week)

Shiai points: 7

Promotion test score: An average of 8

Shichihon-no-kuzushi (the seven off-balance techniques)
Nage-waza (throwing techniques)
(1) Jodan-aigamae-nage-waza (upper regular stance throwing technique) 120
(2) Jodan-gyakugamae-nage-waza (upper reverse stance throwing technique) 122
(3) Chudan-aigamae-nage-waza (middle regular stance throwing technique) 123
(4) Chudan-gyakugamae-nage-waza (middle reverse stance throwing technique) 124
(5) Gedan-aigamae-nage-waza (lower regular stance throwing technique) 125
(6) Gedan-gyakugamae-nage-waza (lower reverse stance throwing technique) 126
(7) Ushiro-ryote-mochi-nage-waza (rear both hands grasp throwing technique) 127

From 2nd kyu to 1st kyu - Brown Belt and Red Stripe

Time in grade: Minimum of three months practice (twice a week)

Shiai points: 8

Promotion test score: An average of 8.2

Ura-waza-no-kata (counterattacks for kihon-no-kata)
(1) Shomen-ate-no-ura (counterattack for shomen-ate) 90
(2) Aigamae-ate-no-ura (counterattack for aigamae-ate) 92
(3) Gyakugamae-ate-no-ura (counterattack for gyakugamae-ate) 94
(4) Gedan-ate-no-ura (counterattack for gedan-ate) 96
(5) Ushiro-ate-no-ura (counterattack for ushiro-ate) 98

Tanto-ni-taisuru Kihon-no-kata (the knife techniques corresponding to the 17 basic techniques)
1. Shomen-ate 144
2. Aigamae-ate 145
3. Gyakugamae-ate 146
4. Gedan-ate 147
5. Ushiro-ate 148
6. Oshi-taoshi 149
7. Ude-gaeshi 150

8. Hiki-taoshi 151
9. Ude-hineri 152
10. Waki-gatame 153

From 1st kyu to Shodan - 1st Degree Black Belt

Time in grade: Minimum of 1 year practice (twice a week)

Shiai points: 9

Promotion test score: An average of 8.5

Ura-waza-no-kata (counterattacks for kihon-no-kata)
(6) Oshi-taoshi-no-ura (counterattack for oshi-taoshi) 100
(7) Hiki-taoshi-no-ura (counterattack for hiki-taoshi) 102
(8) Kote-gaeshi-no-ura (counterattack for kote-gaeshi) 104
(9) Tenkai-kote-hineri-no-ura (counterattack for tenkai-kote-hineri) 106
(10) Tenkai-kote-gaeshi-no-ura (counterattack for tenkai-kote-gaeshi) 108

Tanto-ni-taisuru Kihon-no-kata (the knife techniques corresponding to the 17 basic techniques)
11. Kote-hineri 154
12. Kote-gaeshi 155
13. Tenkai-kote-hineri 156
14. Tenkai-kote-gaeshi 157
15. Mae-otoshi 158
16. Sumi-otoshi 159
17. Hiki-otoshi 160

Both arms against both hands
1. Shomen-oshi
2. Joge-oshi
3. Ushiro-tori-1
4. Ushiro-tori-2
5. Ude-hineri
6. Ude-gaeshi

Throwing techniques
1. Ippon-seoi-nage (one- arm shoulder throw)

From Shodan to Nidan - 2nd Degree Black Belt

Time in grade: Minimum of 2 year practice (twice a week)

Shiai points: 10

Promotion test score: An average of 9

Koryu-goshin-no-kata (self-defense form of traditional aikido)
Suwari-waza (kneeling techniques)
1. Shomen-uchi (frontal strike)
2. Yokomen-uchi (side strike)
3. Tsuki-komi (thrust)
4. Ryote-tori (both hands grasp)
5. Ushiro-kubi-shime (rear strangle)
6. Tekubi-tori (wrist grasp)
7. Sode-tori (sleeve grasp)
8. Mae-eri-tori (lapel grasp)

Tachi-waza (standing techniques)
1. Mae-eri-tori (front lapel grasp)
2. Tekubi-tori (wrist grasp)
3. Sode-tori (sleeve grasp)
4. Tekubi-tori (wrist grasp)
5. Mae-kubi-shime (front neck choke)
6. Ushiro-kubi-shime (rear neck choke)
7. Ushiro-kakae (rear pick up)
8. Eri-tori-hiki-taoshi (grasp lapel and pull down)

Aiki-goshin-ho (aiki self-defense method)
1. Shomen-uchi (head strike) 182
2. Hidari-yokomen-uchi (side face strike) 183
3. Chudan-tsuki (middle thrust) 185

Throwing techniques
2. Koshi-guruma (hip wheel)

Staff techniques
1. Furi-age
2. Furi-oroshi
3. Morote-tsuki

Class D referee certificate

From Nidan to Sandan - 3rd Degree Black Belt

Time in grade: Minimum of three years practice (twice a week)

Shiai points: 12

Promotion test score: An average of 9.2

Koryu-goshin-no-kata (self-defense form of traditional aikido)
Tanto-ni-taisuru-waza (against knife techniques)
1. Shomen-kiri (frontal knife cut)
2. Hidari-yokomen-kiri (left face knife cut)
3. Migi-yokomen-kiri (right face knife cut)
4. Kamae-tsuki (preparation knife thrust)
5. Waki-tsuki (side body knife thrust)
6. Tsuki-komi (knife thrust)
7. Waki-gamae (side knife preparation)
8. Jodan-kiri (upper knife cut)

Aiki-goshin-ho (aiki self-defense method)
4. Jodan-tsuki (upper thrust) 186
5. Mae-geri (front kick) 188
6. Mawashi-geri (round kick) 189
7. Yoko-geri (side kick) 191
8. Ushiro-geri (rear kick) 192

Shichihon-no-kuzushi (the seven off-balance techniques)
Ura-waza (countertechniques)
1. Jodan-aigamae-ura-waza (upper regular stance countertechnique) 128
2. Jodan-gyakugamae-ura-waza (upper reverse stance countertechnique 131
3. Chudan-aigamae-ura-waza (middle regular stance countertechnique) 133
4. Chudan-gyakugamae-ura-waza (middle reverse stance countertechnique) 135
5. Gedan-aigamae-ura-waza (lower regular stance countertechnique) 137
6. Gedan-gyakugamae-ura-waza (lower reverse stance countertechnique) 139
7. Ushiro-ryote-mochi-ura-waza (rear both hands grasp countertechnique) 141

Throwing techniques
3. Kuchiki-taoshi (dead-tree down)

Sword techniques
Basic sword techniques

Class C referee certificate

From Yodan and up need special promotion requirements

XI PROMOTIONS AND SHIAI RECORDS

Name:_____

Telephone_____, Birth date:_____

Address:_____

Note: Instructor must sign each promotion event in this book for rank to be valid.

Beginning
    Date:
    Shiai points and date:
    Signature of instructor:
_____ Place:

8th kyu yellow belt
    Date:
    Shiai points: and date:
    Signature of instructor:
_____ Place:

7th kyu yellow belt red stripe
    Date:
    Shiai points and date:
    Signature of instructor:
_____ Place:

6th kyu green belt
    Date:
    Shiai points and date:
    Signature of instructor:
_____ Place:

5th kyu green belt red stripe
    Date:
    Shiai points and date:
    Signature of instructor:
_____ Place:

4th kyu purple belt
    Date:
    Shiai points and date:
    Signature of instructor:
    Place:

3rd kyu purple belt red stripe
    Date:
    Shiai points and date:
    Signature of instructor:
    Place:

2nd kyu brown belt
    Date:
    Shiai points and date:
    Signature of instructor:
    Place:

1st kyu brown belt red stripe
    Date:
    Shiai points and date:
    Signature of instructor:
    Place:

Shodan (1st degree black belt)
    Date:
    Shiai points and date:
    Signature of instructor:
    Place:

Nidan (2nd degree black belt)
    Date:
    Shiai points and date:
    Signature of instructor:
    Place:

Sandan (3rd degree black belt)
    Date:
    Shiai points and date:
    Signature of instructor:
    Place:

Yodan (4th degree black belt)
    Date:
    Shiai points and date:
    Signature of instructor:
    Place:

Godan (5th degree black belt)
    Date:
    Shiai points and date:
    Signature of instructor:
    Place:

Rokudan (6th degree black belt)
     Date:
     Shiai points and date:
     Signature of instructor:
     Place:

Shichidan (7th degree black belt)
     Date:
     Shiai points and date:
     Signature of instructor:
     Place:

Hachidan (8th degree black belt)
     Date:
     Shiai points and date:
     Signature of instructor:
     Place:

Index

You force your opponent off-balance by pushing without actually grasping him/her
You force your opponent off-balance by pushing without actually grasping him/her 35

BIBLIOGRAPHY

Aida, Hikoichi. Judo-nyumon.Tokyo: Kabushiki-kaisha Aikodo, 1970

Bucher, Charles A. Foundations of Physical Education. 6th ed. Saint Louis: the C.V. Mosby Co., 1972.

Daigo, Toshiro. Judo-kyoshitsu. Tokyo: Kabushiki-kaisha Taishukan-shoten, 1970.

Higashi, Nobuyoshi. School Judo. Tokyo: Kabushiki-kaisha Seibun-do-shoten, 1963.

_____. Kokushiryu Jujitsu. 2nd ed. New York: International Kokushiryu Goshinho Jujitsu Association, 1981.

_____. Karate-do. New York: Kokushi Budo Institute of New York, Inc., 1983.

_____. Basic Judo. New York: The New York Branch of Kokushikan University Press, 1984.

Inoue, Takeshi. Aikido-kata-no-subete. Tokyo: Takeshi Inoue, 1969.

Lee, Ah Loi. Tomiki Aikido - Book One - randori. London Lee, Ah Loi, 1979.

_____. Tomiki Aikido - Book Two. London: Lee, Ah Loi, 1979.

Kodokan. Kodokan Judo. Tokyo: Kodansha, 1963.

_____. Illustrated Kodokan Judo. Tokyo: Kodansha, 1963.

Kudo, Kazuzo. Dynamic Judo - Throwing Techniques. Tokyo, San Francisco, and New York: Japan Publications Trading Company, 1967.

Matsuda, Ryuchi. Hiden Nihon Jujitsu. Tokyo: Kabushiki-kaisha Shinjinbutsu-ouraisha, 1978.

Matsumoto, Y., and others. "A study of the metsuke (aspect of the eyes) in Judo," Bulletin of the Association for the Scientific Studies on Judo. Tokyo: Kodokan, Report IV, 1972.

Ogawa, S., and others. "Studies on Kansetsu waza,"Bullet in of the Association for the Scientific Studies on Judo.Tokyo: Kodokan, Report II, 1963.

Saito, Morihiro. Aikido - Sword, Stick, Body arts, Volume I- Basic Techniques. Translated by William F. Witt. Tokyo: Minato Research & Publishing Company, 1973.

Shigeoka, Noboru. Zenkai Nihon-kendo-kata. Tokyo: Kabushiki-kaisha Ski Journal, 1982.

Shioda, Gohzo. Aikido-nyumon. Tokyo: Kabushiki-kaisha Tsuru-shobo, 1967.

Suzuki, Masao. Kendo-no-naraikata. Tokyo: Kabushiki-kaisha Kinensha, 1972.

Tomiki, Kenji. Aikido-nyumon. Tokyo: Baseball Magazine Sha, 1958.

_____. Shin Aikido Text. Tokyo: Kabushiki-kaisha Tomondo, 1963.

_____. Judo and Aikido. Tokyo: Japan Travel Bureau, Inc, 1956.

_____. Goshinjutsu-nyumon. Tokyo: Kabushiki-kaisha Seito-sha, 1973.

Tomiki, Kenji, Hideo Ohba, and Fumiaki Shishida. Aikido-kyugi-no-tebiki Shin Aikido Text. Kaitei-ban. Tokyo: Kabushiki Kaisha Tomondo, 1984.

Tohei, Koichi. Aikido - The arts of self-defense. Japan: Rikugei Publishing House, 1960.

_____. What is Aikido? Tokyo: Rikugei Publishing House, 1962.

Uyeshiba, Kisshomaru. Aikido. Translated by Kazuaki anahashi, and Roy Maurer Jr. Tokyo: Hozansha Publishing Co., Ltd., 1974.

_____. Aikido-nyumon. Tokyo: Kabushiki-kaisha Kobunsha, 1972.

_____. Aikido-hiyo. Tokyo: Kabushiki-kaisha Tokyo-shoten, 1978.

Yamada, Yoshimitsu. Aikido Complete. New York: Lyle Stuart, Inc., 1969.